Laure Chémery

Weather
and Climates

CHAMBERS
World Library

Contents

✹ Maps

Foreword

Weather and climates influence the development of all life on Earth and, over the long term, help to shape the contours of the planet's surface. Cold, heat, rain, drought and wind all have an impact on the way people live, affecting their food, their dress, their living conditions and how they move about the planet.

Nowadays we sometimes forget the importance of climate and look to technological developments to help free us from its constraints. Whenever an unexpected climatic event occurs, we are often amazed to discover that our immediate environment still depends very much on the whims of the weather.

Climate disruption causes even more concern, with scientists warning both politicians and the public of the risk of global climate change. Human activity is changing the composition of the atmosphere, and this could lead to global warming with repercussions on all aspects of climate, and life on Earth. It is therefore of the utmost importance to have an understanding of climate and the factors that influence it.

Climate can be considered in terms of different timescales (days, seasons, years, millennia) and in terms of different spatial scales (macroclimates, involving entire continents, or microclimates, on the scale of a street or a plant). The constantly moving atmosphere, the Sun with its heat and energy, and water, so essential to life – all of these shape the climate as we know it.

Meteorologists and climatologists the world over are dedicated to gathering information which will allow them to anticipate climatic events and make forecasts. Data is collected by measuring stations and observation satellites and is used to forecast the weather as well as to arrive at a better understanding of past, present and future climates. The careful application of this knowledge is of great benefit to our society and to the rest of the world.

This group of storm clouds over the Pacific Ocean was photographed by the Columbia space shuttle in 1990. Some of the cumulonimbuses are shaped like anvils, a typical feature of these clouds, which can sometimes be more than 15km from top to bottom.

C limate is sometimes difficult to talk about, with its abstract notions of wind, temperature and pressure. In order to make it more concrete and to bring together all the complex elements that make up the climate of a place, climatologists and geographers have established classifications for climate according to various uses and purposes (agroclimatology, bioclimatology, and so on). These classifications, which distinguish about twenty climate types, are only an imperfect reflection of climate in all its diversity, since climatic variations, extremes, anomalies and catastrophes are usually obscured by the use of averages.

The pictures provided by weather satellites are perfect for observing phenomena such as cyclones, depressions or cloud formations (seen here over the coast of South Africa).

Climate: a global patchwork

Scales of climate

There is an important difference between the climatic conditions on the surface of a leaf and those of a whole continent, or between the climate of the Middle Ages and that of distant geological time.

From planet to pasture

Generally, we think of climate as operating on four spatial scales, with the smaller scales dependent on the larger. First, when we talk about an equatorial climate or a temperate climate, we are talking about 'macroclimates' which correspond to vast geographical areas of several million to several tens of millions of square kilometres: a continent, an ocean, a large country, even an entire planet. On this scale, general atmospheric circulation and astronomical factors play a predominant role, but important geographical factors such as oceans and mountain ranges also have to be taken into account.

Secondly, to talk about the climate of the Atlantic coast of Europe or the Iberian peninsula, for example, we would use the term 'mesoclimate' (or regional climate). This denotes a smaller area – between a few thousand and a few tens of thousands of square kilometres – which is defined by its geographical features (basins, mountain ranges, coastal areas, etc). On this scale, it is atmospheric movement and features such as lakes, sea or vegetation that are most important.

Thirdly, the term 'topoclimate' (or local climate) is applied to areas measured in square kilometres or tens of square kilometres: valleys, edges of lakes, towns and forests. Here, it is topography and the nature of the soil that are the dominant influences: they determine phenomena such as breezes, which are not significant at the higher scales.

Finally, a 'microclimate' refers to an area of between a few square centimetres and a few tens of square metres: this is the scale of a farm pasture or a street. In this case, factors such as roughness, shade and obstacles to the wind play an important role.

Situated directly above the equator, seven satellites circle the Earth in an orbit parallel to the equatorial plane and at the same angular velocity as the Earth. Known as 'geostationary', they provide images that enable us to study large areas.

In the course of a summer's day, a field of cereals gives back to the atmosphere several tonnes of water per hectare. The climatic conditions of a cornfield, and even the conditions on the surface of a leaf, are of interest to climatologists.

A year or one million years

Reconstructing climate

Various methods are used to study climate. For the earliest periods, analysis of rocks or sediments, on land or in the ocean, enables scientists to reconstruct the intensity of erosion, the sea levels and the typical vegetation of the time.

For more recent periods, studies are made of soil, ice, lake sediments and what has been trapped in them: dust, pollen or (in glaciers) air bubbles, which are found using probes. For periods close to our own, coral deposits and tree rings provide clues to environmental conditions such as temperature of sea water, amounts of rainfall and air temperature. Written documents go back only 5,000 years, and measuring with instruments goes back only a century or two.

Climate also varies according to different timescales. On a geological timescale, we are able to study 'palaeoclimates' – ancient climates that are between a few hundred and several million years old. The historical timescale covers the period for which we have written archives available.

Using these documents (texts or engravings), a fairly continuous narrative can be pieced together. Finally, the study of present-day climate relies on meteorological measurements, which in some cases date back 150 years.

Generally, measurements taken over a 30-year period are used for defining reference climates and studying short-term variability.

Map (following pages)

Numerous measurements and observations are required for the classification of climates. Some classifications are based on empirical methods (observation of vegetation or meteorological measurements, for example), whereas others, known as 'genetic', are based on atmospheric circulation or the analysis of air masses. This map belongs to the first category.

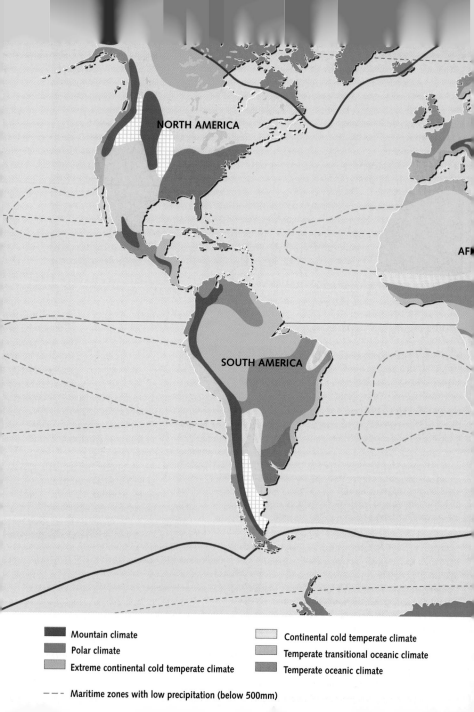

NORTH AMERICA

AF

SOUTH AMERICA

Mountain climate

Polar climate

Extreme continental cold temperate climate

Continental cold temperate climate

Temperate transitional oceanic climate

Temperate oceanic climate

– – – Maritime zones with low precipitation (below 500mm)

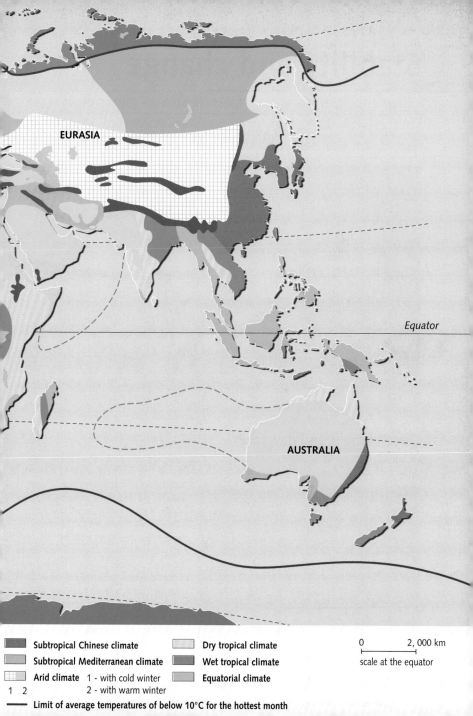

EURASIA

AUSTRALIA

Equator

	Subtropical Chinese climate			Dry tropical climate
	Subtropical Mediterranean climate			Wet tropical climate
	Arid climate 1 - with cold winter			Equatorial climate
1 2	2 - with warm winter			

0   2, 000 km

scale at the equator

── Limit of average temperatures of below 10°C for the hottest month

Stability and change

There is no such thing as a stable climate: all the different regions of the Earth have experienced major environmental variation in geological and even historical times.

This painting from 1608 illustrates the cooling of the climate that was experienced in Europe from 1550 onwards. Paintings and etchings are a good source of information for climate historians, enabling them to reconstruct the conditions of past times.

Development and deviation

Climatologists try to establish mean values for describing climate that are based on long periods of observation. How these reference values change over time are of great interest, as are any deviations from them. These changes are described in terms of range, length, frequency and form (random, cyclical) and in relation to the mean climate that has been defined. We can distinguish two main types of variation: first of all, variations where there is an understandable pattern; and second, anomalies which seem to be random, and for which we have neither data covering a sufficiently long period nor the theoretical tools which would enable us to understand their causes.

Climate in Europe

Ever since written documents have been available, it has been possible to identify two cold periods in the history of Europe: during the Roman period, between AD 0 and AD 400, and after the Middle Ages, between 1550 and 1850. During this latter mini-ice age, with its long hard winters and cool damp summers, it is estimated that the average global temperature was 1-2°C below what it is now. Since 1850, a trend towards a warming of the climate has been observed, but we do not yet know if this is related to human activity.

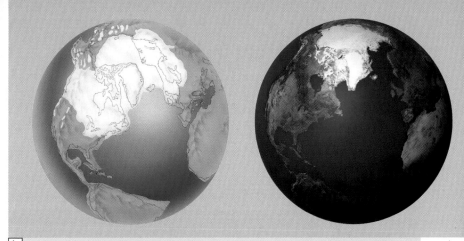

These pictures show the extent of the Arctic icecaps, at present (on the right) and 18,000 years ago (on the left) at the time of the last glacial maximum: most of Eurasia and America were then covered in ice. Some more northerly places, however, like the Bering Strait between Asia and America, were free of ice and even of water: because the icecaps were larger, the sea level was lower.

Trends and oscillations

Trends are variations over time which are not cyclical. Nowadays, we speak about the trend 'towards global warming'. Trend analysis demonstrates the difficulty in choosing a reference period: for example, if the glaciation process were not understood in full, the cooling phase might be called a 'trend'. Oscillations are repetitive, alternating variations of a cyclical nature, but their periodic nature is difficult to prove (the El Niño phenomenon is an example of this).

Cycles and changes

Cycles are more or less regular climatic changes, with a return to the initial conditions between each cycle. The seasons of the year constitute a cycle, as do the day and night. Some long cycles are more difficult to detect: for example, glacial cycles, which unfold over several millennia. One of the main causes of climatic cycles is the variation in the solar energy that reaches the Earth's surface. 4.5 billion years ago, the energy emitted by the Sun was less than 25% of what it is now. Some cycles of solar activity are well understood: for example, the eleven-year sunspot cycle.

For its part, the Earth undergoes shifts in its orbit or rotation over very long periods, and these shifts affect the way in which the Sun's rays are intercepted. The climate may also be altered if the composition of the atmosphere or the nature of the Earth's surface changes – something which may occur as the result of volcanic, biological, human or other processes.

Climate disruption

Each year, climate disruption in the form of floods, droughts, cyclones or storms affects thousands, if not millions, of people and devastates entire regions.

Climatic catastrophes

When climate deviates from the norm, it is the most dramatic climatic events that remain in people's minds. The common factor in these natural crises – which can be brief or long-lasting, local or global, and often random (and therefore difficult to forecast) – is that they are difficult to understand and put the environment and human life under great stress. If such crises or anomalies recur too often, they may signal a long-term change in the reference climate. However, sufficient time needs to elapse before it can be determined that climate change has definitely taken place.

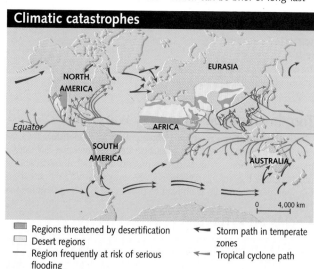

Climatic catastrophes

NORTH AMERICA

EURASIA

Equator

AFRICA

SOUTH AMERICA

AUSTRALIA

0   4,000 km

- ▬ Regions threatened by desertification
- ▭ Desert regions
- — Region frequently at risk of serious flooding
- ◄— Storm path in temperate zones
- ◄— Tropical cyclone path

Dust bowl

In the 1930s, the vast wheat-growing plains of the central and southern USA experienced a climatic phenomenon known as 'dust bowl'. Poor land use (intensive ploughing, increased numbers of livestock, and abandoning the practice of leaving the land fallow) resulted in the ground becoming bare in places. Evaporation was reduced and rainfall decreased. Strong winds removed the dry earth and exposed the rock underneath, thus preventing further cultivation. The huge exodus which followed was recounted by John Steinbeck in his 1939 novel *The Grapes of Wrath*.

Harmful to humans and detrimental to their environment

Only those anomalies that are harmful to humans or detrimental to their activities and their environment are known as 'climatic catastrophes'.

Thus, an extensive drought may have an impact on the natural environment, but if it occurs in an uninhabited region it is rarely designated a climatic catastrophe. Since regions devoid of humans or human activity are becoming increasingly rare, and those regions that are inhabited are becoming more vulnerable, it is generally considered that the number of climatic catastrophes is on the increase. This trend is likely to continue but it is not necessarily a sign that climatic anomalies are increasing in frequency or scale.

Forecasting and preventive measures, together with emergency plans, can stop a climatic anomaly from turning into a catastrophe. In rich countries, risk exposure has been only a minor consideration for the last few decades, but it is now being taken seriously again, in development planning and elsewhere. At the same time, the risks are becoming less and less acceptable to people. In poor countries, the risk of catastrophe is often considerable as a result of underdevelopment.

In rich countries, the nature of the damage is mostly economic: the total cost of the flooding in central and eastern Europe in the summer of 2002 (seen here in Prague) is estimated at 2 to 3 billion euros for the Czech Republic and 15 billion euros for Germany.

Too much or too little rain, wind, heat or cold

Heavy precipitation can cause flooding, which is responsible for some of the greatest human catastrophes as well as causing considerable economic damage. Excessive snowfall or hailstorms sometimes have a great human or economic impact, too, particularly on agriculture. Another form of rainfall anomaly is drought, which also causes human and/or economic damage. However, droughts take longer to build up than floods.

Too much wind, creating storms, cyclones and tornadoes, is another potential force for destruction. However, with better forecasting of these events, it is possible to safeguard lives by advising people of the precautionary measures they need to take. The main consequences then take the form of material and economic damage.

As for extremes of temperature (whether hot or cold), they often result in catastrophes which are less spectacular than those caused by wind or rain, although they too may be harmful to human life and health.

Although some weather phenomena are part of the variable climate (such as the effects of drought as seen here), they can nevertheless cause great hardship. Loss of life is minimal, but there is an increase in social, psychological, economic and technical vulnerability.

Analysing and forecasting

Measuring stations and observation satellites are permanently studying the Earth's atmosphere. The data obtained is used to forecast weather and describe climate.

Measurements on the ground

Climate research is based on the observations and measurements obtained from a network of meteorological stations. There are around 9,000 of these, and the main ones measure the basic atmospheric parameters at least twice a day: temperature, precipitation, atmospheric pressure, air humidity, wind direction and strength, and amount of sunlight. Qualitative observations are also carried out on storms, cloud types, extent of snow or cloud cover, ice floes, and so on. In addition to these, there are automated stations, connected to a computer by telephone or satellite link, that provide measurements in places where access is difficult, such as mountains, deserts and oceans. In the ocean, measuring is done over a wide area: there are 4,000 merchant ships, specialized ships and automated stations attached to fixed or free-floating buoys, providing regular data.

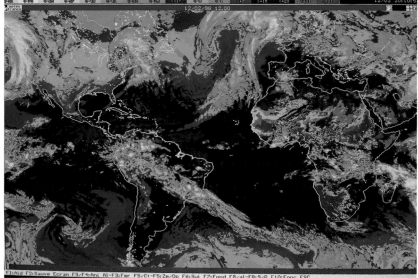

Satellites provide pictures of objects that are visible to the naked eye, such as clouds, and also measurements of infrared radiation, which is closer to thermal than to visible radiation.

High-altitude measurements

In addition to the measurements carried out on the Earth's surface, about 900 stations throughout the world release weather balloons to measure temperature, pressure, air humidity and so on at high altitude. A radar network and a satellite network complete the system. The radar enables precipitation to be observed, and every 30 minutes, five geostationary satellites provide a complete picture of the cloud cover and the humidity and temperature of the Earth's atmosphere. There are also a few satellites that specialize in observing oceans or vegetation.

Throughout the world, nearly 9,000 stations, run by specialized personnel, form part of the World Meteorological Network (pictured here is the Mauna Loa observatory in Hawaii). Their data is supplemented by additional data from 130,000 reporting stations, which are mostly run by voluntary staff.

Processing the data

Once meteorological data has been obtained, it is collected, centralized and analysed. One of the main objectives of the analysis is forecasting the weather, and the best-known aid for this is the weather chart. The data provided by the network of stations is used to construct the isobars and fronts, and in this way areas of high and low pressure and disturbances are highlighted. These charts are produced both for the Earth's surface and for different levels of altitude, and it is by interpreting them that weather forecasters can anticipate the weather. Climatologists, on the other hand, use the same data to try and establish a reference climate.

Creating a forecasting model

Powerful computers have the dual task of processing the data collected and creating models: these are simplified representations of the atmosphere, using the laws of physics and earlier observations. For the meteorologist, the purpose is to predict how a situation will evolve over several hours or days; the climatologist, however, is concerned with determining, over a longer timescale, what the atmosphere's response would be if one of the parameters were to change (atmospheric composition, supply of solar energy, or inclination of the Earth's axis, for example).

The WMO

The World Meteorological Organization, created in 1947, lays down measuring guidelines and co-ordinates the international network of stations. The world is organized into five regions and each country transmits the observations carried out on its territory to the relevant region. These 'continental measurements' are then transmitted to other participating countries so that they can make their forecasts.

Climate: a global patchwork **19**

The uses of climatology

Climate research is of major relevance to the many human activities that are affected by atmospheric conditions. Among these activities are transport, agriculture, housing and construction.

Transport

Transport, and in particular navigation, has long been dependent on climate. The Ancient Greeks' sophisticated description of winds in the Mediterranean Basin reflects the importance of climate for a people who used sailing ships extensively. Today we are still dependent on climate, though the invention of radar has meant that we are able to protect ourselves from danger (cumulonimbus clouds, cyclones, freezing fog) and take advantage of favourable conditions – transatlantic flights between New York and London make use of jet streams flowing from west to east, enabling them to cut journey times and reduce energy consumption.

Hedges are used to protect land under cultivation, as here in the Rhône valley, which is exposed to the mistral, a strong cold dry wind blowing mainly in winter. The effectiveness of a hedge is measured in terms of the reduction of wind speed and the size of the area protected.

Agroclimatology

Agriculture is extremely sensitive to those elements of climate that are important for plant life: rain, sunshine and temperature. A lack of rain can be partly compensated for by pumping water into the ground or by the soil absorbing the water that is present in the atmosphere, until such time as both of these are themselves affected by the absence of rain. Increasingly, agriculture is developing various means of correcting the climate: greenhouses allow a higher ambient temperature to be maintained; irrigation and drainage networks overcome the problems of irregular rainfall; and hedges help to reduce wind speed. One of the jobs of the climatologist is to try and assess the profitability of such high-cost investments.

Housing

Since the purpose of houses is to protect humans

In order to capture wind energy, sites are needed which are exposed to winds that are preferably regular and strong. Generally speaking, the energy potential of the various elements of climate (sunshine, rainfall stored behind electric dams, etc) is considerable.

from the rigours of the climate so that they can live comfortably, the science of bioclimatology is of great relevance to house-building techniques. Nowadays, building concerns are influenced by energy issues: buildings must be comfortable but at the same time low in energy consumption. The shape of buildings and roofs, the direction the house faces, the size of doors and windows, the materials used, whether the house has a porch or sun lounge, whether it is built on piles – all these are features of traditional architecture that have been taken over and reinterpreted by bioclimatic architecture, which also makes use of technological innovations such as double glazing, filter glass, aerated concrete and various insulating and waterproofing materials.

Dependent on climate

The agribusiness industry is dependent on climate at both ends of the chain, from the agricultural produce that supplies it to the consumers who buy the end products. Fizzy drinks, beer and ice cream are mostly consumed in summer, whereas meat and pulses tend to be winter foods. The increased consumption of deep-frozen and preserved products indicates that people want to be able to consume seasonal foods all year round. Last but not least, manufacturing processes which require time for a product to ferment (brewing) or mature (cheese production) are extremely dependent on atmospheric conditions.

Economic activities

Many other activities are closely linked to climate, in particular those of the energy industry, which has to gear its production to consumer demand. For example, the amount of gas supplied to consumers in one day varies depending on the season: in winter it might be five times what it is in summer. In warmer regions, how hot it is dictates how often the air conditioning will be used. Tourism, with its expectations of snow in winter and the demand for warmth and sun in summer, is also very dependent on the weather. Insurance to cover weather risks is increasingly in demand.

A changing science

Questions have been asked about the weather since time immemorial, but climatology and meteorology are recent sciences which prompted the development of various scientific instruments.

Observation and measurement

People have always asked questions about the weather. In ancient times, the Mesopotamians, the Egyptians and the Indians described and analysed atmospheric conditions, relying on their religious beliefs to understand them. The Greeks (Aristotle and his treatise *Meteorologics*), the Arabs and the Chinese approached observation rationally and attempted to supply the first explanations of global weather: the Greeks based their explanations of why different regions were dry or wet and warm or cool on differences in the length of the day.

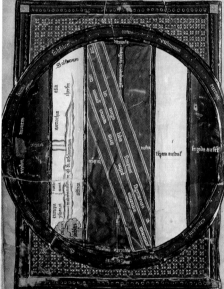

On this manuscript from 1277, the Earth is divided into three broad climatic regions: the torrid zone is coloured red (the equator is represented by the thick vertical line), the temperate zone is white and the cold zone is blue.

An early revolution

It was only when measuring instruments came on the scene that significant progress could be made: in the course of the 17th century, the inventions of Galileo (thermoscope), Torricelli (barometer) and Hooke (hygrometer) allowed temperature, pressure and air humidity respectively to be measured. The first network for standardized measurements was set up in Italy in 1653 by Grand Duke Ferdinand of Florence. An academy was responsible for centralizing the data over a period of about ten years. This type of network was also developed in France and Britain. Halley and then Hadley published the first diagrams showing how atmospheric circulation worked. Taking advantage of advances in navigation, geographers collected new observational data and developed the first classifications of climate. During the 19th century, the first continuously functioning measurement networks were developed.

GLOSSARY

[Model]
Simplified or digitized representation of the atmosphere and its properties, used to forecast weather or simulate climate.

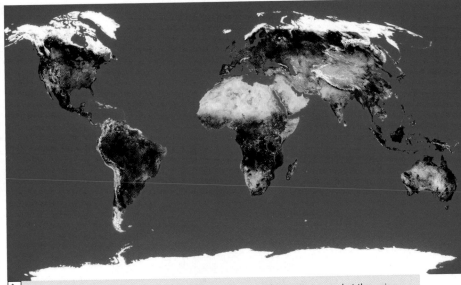

Almost eight centuries separate this picture from the one on the previous page, but the major concern in both is the understanding of climate.

New theories, new technologies

Also during the 19th century, there was a scientific revolution: thermodynamics, fluid mechanics and statistics gave renewed life to the study of atmospheric conditions. Two strands emerged: weather forecasting and climate research. In the latter field, ideas about the unchanging nature of climates and species were abandoned. People learned to interpret geological clues about earlier climates. From 1950 onwards, new methods such as pollen studies, isotope research and polar ice analysis helped with the description of earlier climates.

As for weather forecasting, a great leap forward was made with the appearance of balloons, aircraft and satellites, making high-altitude measurements a common activity. The arrival of computers and the development of telecommunications networks led to the collected data being centralized on a worldwide scale, making it possible to create atmospheric models providing much more detailed forecasts and, more recently, to reconstruct earlier climates.

Military uses

In 1854, during the Crimean war, the French fleet was hit by a storm. The astronomer Le Verrier observed that this storm had crossed the entire continent of Europe, from west to east, in the space of a few days, but that owing to the lack of a communications system, no warning of it could be given. As a result of this disaster, the major powers decided to equip themselves with observational tools and weather-forecasting facilities. A century later, this precaution paid off when the date of the Normandy landings was put back by 24 hours because forecasters had announced strong winds.

The atmosphere – where weather and climate processes occur – is governed by the physical laws of the gases of which it is composed. Air pressure (the weight exerted by a column of atmosphere at each point of the Earth's surface) varies according to geographical position, altitude and the amount of sun that warms the air, making it lighter. Winds are mainly the result of temperature differences in the atmosphere, and their movement tends to compensate for these; they occur mostly in the lower atmosphere.

Satellite imagery has revolutionized the study of the atmosphere: it has now become possible, for the first time, to view whole cloud systems. In this picture, taken at an angle over Africa, the thin layer that makes up the Earth's atmosphere can be seen in the distance.

The restless atmosphere

The vertical structure of the atmosphere

The atmosphere is made up of layers with specific thermal and chemical characteristics. The layer closest to the Earth's surface is the most significant in terms of climatic processes.

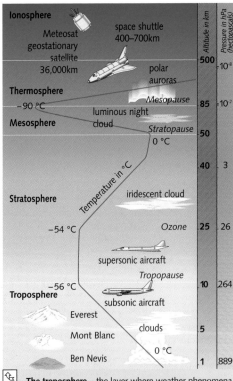

The troposphere – the layer where weather phenomena develop – is 8km thick over the poles and 17km thick over the equator. The stratosphere contains ozone, which absorbs part of the Sun's ultraviolet radiation and thus protects life on Earth. Above that, the mesosphere is where the polar auroras occur, while the thermosphere absorbs X-rays and some ultraviolet radiation.

Nitrogen, oxygen and other gases

Air is present up to more than 750km above the Earth's surface, but most of the processes that determine the weather occur in the first 20 kilometres. In fact, half of the atmosphere's mass is situated less than 5.5km away from the Earth's surface, and 99% is to be found within the lowest 30 kilometres. In the first layer, the homosphere, which extends from the surface up to a height of 90–100km, the chemical composition of the air is fairly constant, with a permanent mix of gases: 78% nitrogen and 21% oxygen.

The other gaseous components (including argon, carbon dioxide, neon, helium, krypton and hydrogen) are present in very small quantities, totalling about 1% of the air. The homosphere also contains solid objects such as dust, salt crystals and volcanic ash, which have come from the Earth. These can be found within the lowest 10 kilometres, except for volcanic ash, which is sometimes projected to as far up as 15km or 20km. In addition, the homosphere contains water vapour in the proportion of 0.1–4% of the volume of dry air, depending on the region.

The next layer of the atmosphere, the

heterosphere, contains light gases like helium and hydrogen, as well as nitrogen. Oxygen is no longer present in its molecular form but is present in its atomic form – this is the ozone layer. Finally, above 750km lies the outermost layer, the exosphere, from which a few particles of helium and hydrogen escape into outer space.

Varying temperatures

Four thermal layers can be identified in the lowest 500km of the atmosphere: beyond that, the air is too rarefied for temperature to be measured. In the troposphere (from the Earth's surface up to 10km), the temperature decreases steadily by 6°C for every 100m until, at the top of the layer, it reaches between -50°C (over the poles) and -80°C (over the equator). The pressure also gradually decreases: from 1,013hPa (hectopascals) on the surface to 400hPa over the poles and

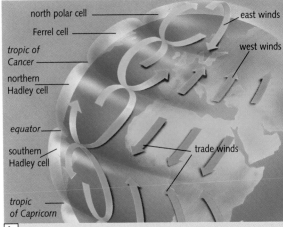

north polar cell

Ferrel cell

tropic of Cancer

northern Hadley cell

equator

southern Hadley cell

tropic of Capricorn

east winds

west winds

trade winds

Exchanges between the air circulation on the Earth's surface and the air circulation at high altitude take the form of 'cells', which link flows of air that are subsiding with flows that are ascending. On the surface, the subsiding flows correspond to high-pressure zones resulting in a divergence of air, whereas the ascending flows correspond to low-pressure zones resulting in a convergence of air.

100hPa over the equator. In the stratosphere (between 10km and 50km), the temperature is constant at around -55°C up to 20km. It then rises, under the effect of the ozone layer, to reach between 0°C and 20°C at around 50km. In the mesosphere (between 50km and 85km), the air becomes thin and the temperature is low: around -90°C at the top of the layer. Measurements are difficult to obtain, but it is thought that in the thermosphere (between 85km and 500km) the temperature can rise to 1,000°C at around 300km.

Vertical movements

Although most movements of the atmosphere are in a horizontal direction, vertical movements also occur. These are due to powerful ascending and subsiding movements of air. It is thought that the troposphere is made up of large 'cells' which follow the general circulation of the atmosphere (both on the Earth's surface and at altitude), combining vertical and horizontal movements and thermal transfer. There are two major cells in each hemisphere: the Hadley cell, situated between 0° and 30°, and the Ferrel cell, between 30° and 60°. Another, less prominent cell is to be found in the high latitudes beyond 60°: this combines a rising movement at middle latitudes with a subsiding movement at the pole.

Map (following pages)

Centres of activity such as the most 'stable' depressions and anticyclones, air masses or disturbances are not permanent or fixed. They form, migrate and develop under the influence of solar energy, the Earth's rotation and relief, and the nature of the surface over which they move (landmass or ocean). It is interesting to compare this atmospheric circulation map for January with the one on page 30, for July.

The restless atmosphere **27**

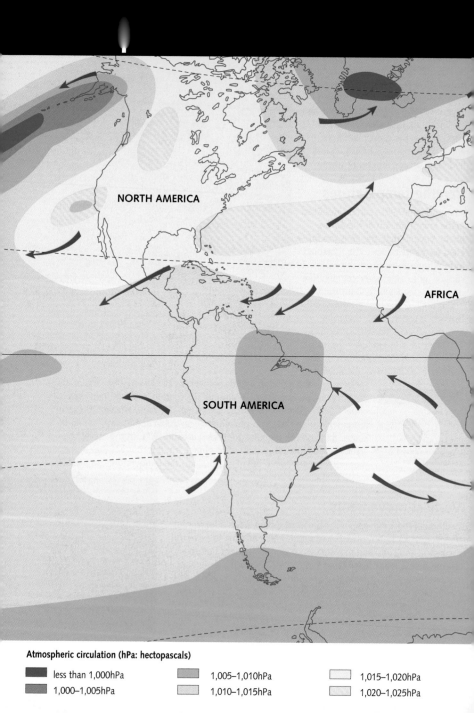

Atmospheric circulation (hPa: hectopascals)

- less than 1,000hPa
- 1,000–1,005hPa
- 1,005–1,010hPa
- 1,010–1,015hPa
- 1,015–1,020hPa
- 1,020–1,025hPa

NORTH AMERICA

SOUTH AMERICA

AFRICA

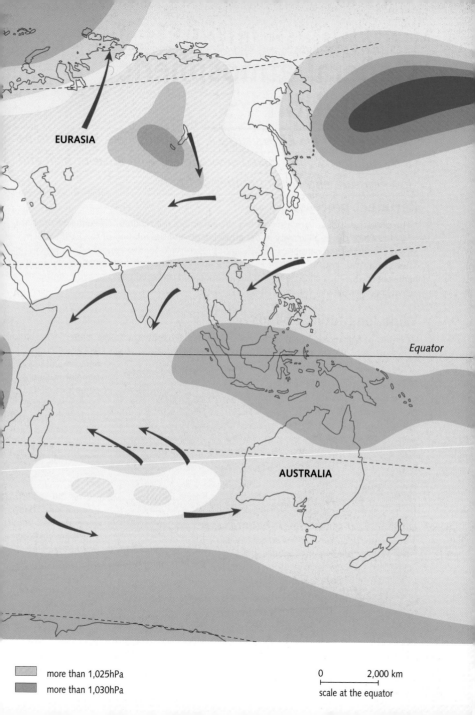

EURASIA

Equator

AUSTRALIA

more than 1,025hPa
more than 1,030hPa

0   2,000 km

scale at the equator

General atmospheric circulation

At the level of the Earth's surface, the atmosphere appears to be a constantly moving, mixed environment with areas of high and low pressure and discontinuities or fronts.

Recurrent processes

The processes that govern atmospheric circulation are not random. The principal ones are sunlight, which drives all activity in the atmosphere, and the rotation of the Earth, which affects movements in centres of activity and is responsible for the Coriolis effect, which causes objects to veer to the right in the northern hemisphere and to the left in the southern hemisphere. It is thus possible to plot the location and preferred paths of large centres of activity, air masses and discontinuities.

Wide longitudinal bands

Centres of activity are organized in wide longitudinal bands around the globe. These bands lie parallel to the equator and symmetrically on either side of it. The location of these centres changes with the seasons, as each hemisphere in turn receives more (and then less) solar energy.

Over the poles, a low-pressure zone generates east winds, which are cold, dry and fast-moving, often reaching 200kph. At middle latitudes, zones of discontinuity are characterized by westerly winds. In the northern hemisphere, westerly

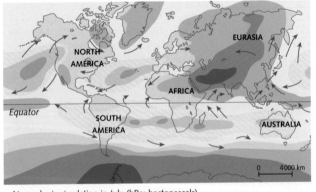

Atmospheric circulation in July (hPa: hectopascals)

■ less than 1,000hPa	☐ 1,010–1,015hPa	▨ more than 1,025hPa
■ 1,000–1,005hPa	☐ 1,015–1,020hPa	■ more than 1,030hPa
■ 1,005–1,010hPa	☐ 1,020–1,025hPa	

0   4 000 km

The amount of solar energy changes with the seasons, benefiting each hemisphere in turn. This affects the general atmospheric circulation: between April and September, the polar depression in the Arctic weakens. The west winds move to higher latitudes and, with them, the anticyclonic belt, which gets as far as 40° N. The intertropical convergence zone also moves towards 10–15° N.

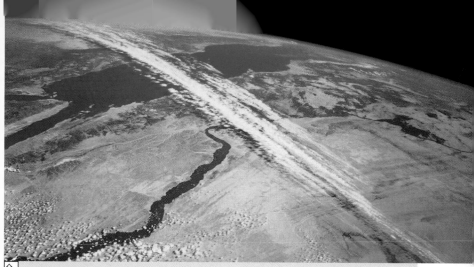

Taken by Gemini 12 in the 1960s, this picture shows the jet stream flowing over east Africa, the Red Sea and the Arabian Peninsula.

winds bring rain to the temperate regions of America and Eurasia; in the southern hemisphere, however, where there are no mountain barriers to slow them down, these winds are often stronger and steadier – the roaring forties and furious fifties, well known to seafarers. At subtropical latitudes, there is a belt of high pressure which includes the anticyclones of the Azores (North Atlantic), Saint Helena (South Atlantic), Easter Island (South Pacific), California (North Pacific), and the archipelago of islands that include Réunion and Mauritius (Indian Ocean). This band of high pressure is notable for its absence of wind. South of this band, strong steady winds, known as the trade winds, converge towards a low-pressure zone, the intertropical convergence zone, which is situated more or less at the equator (between 10° N and 10° S).

GLOSSARY

[Air mass]
An extensive body of air, whose properties (temperature, humidity, etc) are relatively homogeneous.

High altitude

Most of this activity takes place in the troposphere, below 10km. But atmospheric conditions at high altitude also contribute to the general circulation: even though most air movement is horizontal, there are nevertheless exchanges between the Earth's surface and the upper atmosphere.

The stratosphere, above 10km, experiences powerful winds in the form of jet streams. These blow from west to east at latitudes of 30–60°. In winter, they subdivide into two branches. The subtropical jet stream, which is the more persistent and powerful, blows at an altitude of 11–14km and a latitude of around 30°, and its speed can reach 400kph; the polar jet stream blows at an altitude of 9–10km and a latitude of around 60°. In summer, the two currents weaken and move closer together: they are then at an altitude of 10–12km and a latitude of 40–50°.

Anticyclones and depressions

Although atmospheric pressure is not something we can perceive with our senses, it is nevertheless a crucial factor in determining weather. Its uneven distribution is the cause of winds.

Pressure and pressure fields

Atmospheric pressure is measured at the Earth's surface and at various altitudes: the higher the altitude, the lower the pressure. The average pressure is around 1,000hPa (hectopascals) at ground level, around 850hPa at 1,500m, around 200hPa at 12km and around 10hPa at 60km. Pressure also varies horizontally, allowing us to identify areas of high pressure (anticyclones) and areas of low pressure (depressions). Horizontal forces – winds – tend to compensate for these discrepancies.

Anticyclones

In an anticyclone, pressure is high and the air is falling (it is said to be 'subsiding'). This subsidence prevents air rising, and rising air is what creates clouds. The weather is generally fine. There are two permanent high-pressure areas in each hemisphere: the first is situated over the poles and the second at subtropical latitudes. Polar anticyclones are generated by the cold dense stable air over the poles, and are shallow: they disappear at an altitude of around 1,500m and are more intense in winter. Tropical anticyclones correspond to the subsiding flow of the Hadley cell, and form a particularly stable

In order to study pressure fields, barometer readings are transferred to pressure charts prepared in weather stations. This enables meteorologists to draw contours connecting points of equal atmospheric pressure (isobars), of which the main centres are anticyclones and depressions. These areas of maximum and minimum pressure are shown enclosed by lines. Other figures used on charts are: troughs (elongated areas of low pressure), ridges (elongated areas of high pressure), cols (areas of relatively high pressure separating two depressions) and shallow depressions (vast areas with small pressure gradients).

belt over the oceans. Over landmasses, they are more intense in winter because the colder, heavier air is allied to the effect of dynamic subsidence; in summer, when the lower strata experience the warming effect of strong sunshine, tropical anticyclones are milder. There are also more local and seasonal anticyclonic cells: the Siberian anticyclone, for example, occurs in winter as a result of temperature change, and migrating anticyclones are formed in temperate regions due to the effect of waves from the jet stream.

The Torricelli experiment

In 1643, Torricelli, Galileo's former assistant, carried out an experiment which demonstrated the existence of atmospheric pressure. Using a mercury-filled tube, he showed that air had weight. This experiment was the basis for the barometer, an instrument that measures atmospheric pressure.

Depressions

Depressions, or areas of low pressure, are mobile and changeable. The air in them is usually light, and so rises. Semi-permanent areas of low pressure are found at the equator and at a latitude of around 50° or 60° in each hemisphere. At the equator, this corresponds to the ascending flow of the Hadley cell and the warming of the lower layers of the atmosphere. At middle latitudes, the low pressure corresponds to the ascending flow of the Ferrel cell and is situated more or less under the subtropical jet stream. Depressions are caused by air movement, and they may be intensified when they pass over warm sea currents. They are extremely mobile, moving from the south-west in the northern hemisphere and from the north-west in the southern hemisphere. In addition, seasonal depressions are formed in the summer over hot landmasses at tropical and temperate latitudes because of the warm air rising there, and over oceans in the intertropical zone during the hot season (where they are the cause of tropical cyclones).

Movements

Differences in pressure produce compensatory forces in the form of winds. Although they drive many anticyclones towards depressions, these movements are in fact difficult to discern because of the background Coriolis effect. In the northern hemisphere, air turns clockwise around an anticyclone and anticlockwise around depressions. This is reversed in the southern hemisphere.

The high pressure associated with anticyclones makes cloud formation difficult, but it does not totally prevent clouds from forming: the Azores anticyclone is sometimes accompanied by low continuous cloud while the Sahara anticyclone (seen here) allows a few cumulus clouds to break through.

Winds

Winds are a very noticeable climatic feature, the most obvious signs of movement in the atmosphere. They result from uneven atmospheric pressure, for which they try to compensate.

Movements of air ...

In theory, winds should flow directly from areas of high pressure towards areas of low pressure. But the Coriolis effect, caused by the Earth's rotation, alters their course and, in the northern hemisphere, sends them in a clockwise direction around an anticyclone, and in the opposite direction around a depression. In the southern hemisphere, this effect is reversed.

The points of the Earth's surface which have equal atmospheric pressure can be represented by a line linking them, called an 'isobar'. Near the equator, where the Coriolis effect is less active, winds do sometimes flow at right angles to the isobars. Elsewhere, winds moving from anticyclones towards low-pressure areas do so at an angle of 10–15° between isobars over oceans, and at an angle of 30° over landmasses.

windward slope | mountain range | leeward slope

The föhn

The föhn is a warm dry fast wind that blows on the sheltered side of mountainous areas. Known as the 'chinook' in the United States and the 'Afghan wind' in central Asia, this type of wind occurs when humid air along the windward slope of a mountain range cools, causing condensation, clouds and precipitation. Freed from its humidity, the wind blows down the leeward side both drier and warmer, the latent heat having been turned into sensible heat.

GLOSSARY

[Coriolis effect] Alteration of the course of a wind or other moving body, due to the Earth's rotation.

... and energy

Winds move not only enormous air masses but also substantial amounts of energy in the form of latent heat (which has come about due to a substance's change of state) or 'sensible heat' (if there has been no change of state).

On a global scale, wind distribution adds up to a transfer of cold air towards the equator and warm air towards the poles. Winds are characterized by the temperature and humidity of the areas they come from, but they change en route in accordance with the characteristics of the surfaces over which they flow: thus, a wind which was dry to begin with gradually becomes humid if it flows over the ocean for a long time.

The major wind systems

On a global scale, winds are linked to those places that are major centres of activity. For example, the polar east winds, which blow at latitudes above 60, diverge from the polar anticyclone towards more middle latitudes. The westerly winds of the middle latitudes (between 30° and 60°) are linked to the low-pressure belt of these latitudes. The trade winds, which blow from north-east to south-west in the northern hemisphere and from south-east to north-west in the southern hemisphere, diverge from the high-pressure zone of the tropical latitudes and converge on the equatorial low-pressure belt. Monsoons are winds of the

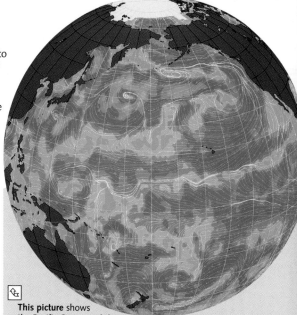

This picture shows the Pacific Ocean and the winds that circulate in it: two typhoons can be seen to the south and east of Japan. These are particularly violent, and will cause severe damage. In the southern hemisphere, the roaring forties and the furious fifties can be seen. Around the equator, on either side of a zone of calm, the trade winds are visible, coloured pink.

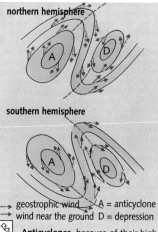

northern hemisphere

southern hemisphere

→ geostrophic wind   A = anticyclone
→ wind near the ground D = depression

Anticyclones, because of their high pressure, tend to drive air away. But this movement is counteracted by the Coriolis effect, linked to the Earth's rotation, which means that moving bodies undergo pressure to veer to the right in the northern hemisphere and to the left in the southern hemisphere.

intertropical zone whose direction changes when they cross the equator. They blow from north to south in winter and in the opposite direction in summer. All of these winds usually change with the seasons: they intensify, they diminish to the point of disappearing altogether, or they move northwards or southwards according to the strength of the centres of activity that govern them. Great mountain ranges like the Rockies or the Andes form barriers, and these have a profound effect on the global system.

On a regional scale, each area has specific winds linked to the local pressure field, which is itself linked to surface conditions: presence of water, glaciers, deserts, relief and so on. It is at higher altitudes, where the influence of relief and roughness on the ground is minimized, that the winds are fastest: jet streams can reach up to 400kph.

Cyclones and tornadoes

These are remarkable demonstrations of atmospheric forces, breaking records for wind speed, barometric pressure and precipitation.

Whirlwind systems

Cyclones and tornadoes are atmospheric whirlwind formations, accompanied by powerful winds. Cyclones form during the hot season over the oceans of the intertropical zone. They measure several hundred kilometres in diameter, have a life span of several weeks and are accompanied by violent rainstorms. Tornadoes are smaller (a few tens of metres in diameter), move very fast and last between a few minutes and a few hours. They occur mostly over hot

On first-name terms with monsters

Since 1953 tropical cyclones have been given a name as a means of identification. The first cyclone of the year in each region is given a name beginning with A, the second a name beginning with B, and so on. Until 1978, the names were exclusively female, but it was then realized that this practice could be considered sexist. Since 1979, names have alternated between male and female.

landmasses. However, some less violent tornadoes occur at sea, and these are called 'waterspouts'.

Cyclones

Known as 'typhoons' when they occur in the western Pacific, cyclones develop over oceans that have been heating up all summer until the water temperature reaches at least 26.5°C down to a depth of several metres.

The lower layers of the atmosphere heat up and air begins to rise, boosted by convergence on the ground and divergence at high altitude, since this is taking place close to the

As long as a cyclone is moving over a warm ocean, it strengthens. When it arrives over a mass of cold water or a landmass, the supplies of warm humid air capable of being transformed into movement are reduced, and the cyclone is permanently weakened. This is probably what is happening to this cyclone arriving over Central America.

intertropical convergence zone.

'Mature' cyclones are between 500km and 1,000km in diameter. The central eye is an area of calm whose diameter (between 10km and 100km) is gradually reduced as the cyclone forms.

The central zone (in which wind speeds can exceed 300kph and the wall of cumulonimbus clouds towers up to 15km high) may vary in diameter between a few tens of kilometres and 200km. The pressure here is very low, there is plentiful rain and a high temperature. The outer zone is 100–200km across and is an area where winds accelerate, feeding the cyclone through its base. The clouds here form spirals around the eye (there may be between two and seven spirals). Cyclones move from east to west at an average speed of 30kph.

eye of the cyclone

winds

eye wall

outer zone

eye wall

precipitation

precipitation

0 50 100 200 250 180 100 50 40
500 400 300 20

distance from the centre in km

wind speed in kph

speed of travel: 30kph

WEST

EAST

As it flows over the warm ocean, air becomes charged with water vapour which cools and condenses as it rises: this releases a considerable amount of energy which is transformed into movement at the heart of the cyclone. The central depression (the eye of the cyclone) draws air in from the periphery and causes it to rise in a whirlwind.

On average, about 40 occur each year. Forecasting and protective measures are the only means of guarding against the damage they cause.

Waterspouts are tornadoes which occur at sea. It is very rare to see a double one, as in this photograph (taken in south-western France on 17 October 2002).

Tornadoes

Tornadoes form when there are substantial differences in temperature between the warm humid air on the Earth's surface and the very cold air of the high troposphere, at an altitude of around 10km. The warm humid air rises suddenly, then cools and condenses, and a cloudy whirlwind forms. Often resulting from storms and violent winds, a tornado looks like a funnel-shaped column (a 'tuba') descending from a cumulonimbus towards the Earth's surface. The colour of the tuba depends on the dust whipped up from the ground. It makes a roaring noise, similar to that of an aeroplane or train. Tornadoes are small, have a limited life span and develop over distances of a few dozen kilometres. They are also difficult to predict. They generate the strongest winds in the world, reaching up to 500kph. In fact, their speed is impossible to measure precisely: instead, they are assessed on the basis of the damage they cause.

Interaction between ocean and atmosphere

Mild temperatures, high rainfall, strong and frequent winds – the ocean has a significant influence on the regions bordering it, as well as on the atmosphere in general.

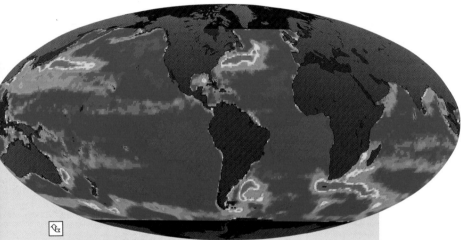

Solar energy, the Earth's
rotation and winds are the main forces influencing the movement of the oceans.
These forces are modified by underwater relief, temperature and water salinity.
In this artificially coloured picture, warm currents like the Gulf Stream can be
seen in yellow and red, and cold currents like the Humboldt Current off the
coast of South America are coloured purple.

Capacity for storing energy

The seas and oceans cover more than 71% of the Earth's surface, and 97% of the Earth's water is concentrated in them. The atmosphere can be enriched with water vapour through a process of evaporation from this gigantic reservoir. The oceans also regulate temperature, as sea currents move hot masses of water from the equator towards the poles and glacial masses towards the equator. The quantities of energy transferred are even greater than that, since the oceans, being so big, receive a large share of the Sun's energy, which they are able to store by absorbing it. Last but not least, ocean currents move water masses (and therefore heat reserves) over much greater distances and with much greater efficiency than atmospheric currents, which transfer energy into one air mass after another.

Transfer of energy

Thus, the circulation of the ocean plays an important role in transferring heat between hot and cold regions. The energy is then returned to the atmosphere, either in the form of sensible heat through contact between air mass and ocean, or in the form of latent heat by means of water vapour. While transferring energy to regions that are sometimes a long way away, the surface currents have a marked influence on climate: for example, the effect of the Gulf Stream is to make the temperatures on the west coast of Europe considerably milder. The influence is sometimes more complex: the Humboldt Current along the coast of Peru brings about a cooling of the lower layers of the atmosphere, preventing cloud formation and therefore precipitation. The coastline is consequently very barren.

Complex interactions

The El Niño phenomenon (first mentioned in manuscripts going back to the 17th century) plays a particular role in the complex relationship between atmosphere and ocean. In certain years the surface waters along the Peruvian coastline reach a peak of warming in December, and torrential rain ensues. Only recently have scientists understood that this sea current, El Niño, causes a disturbance in the general atmospheric circulation, with repercussions across the whole planet, especially in the intertropical zone. As a result, we see droughts in some regions but dramatic flooding elsewhere; tropical cyclones are more numerous, while Indian monsoons are less severe.

The speed of sea currents

Deep currents move slowly: it is thought that 1,000 years are needed for water to travel from the depths of the North Atlantic to the current around the South Pole. Surface currents are usually faster: those linked to the trade winds travel 60km a day, and the fastest current recorded, the Somali Current, can travel 250km a day.

A year with and without 'El Niño'

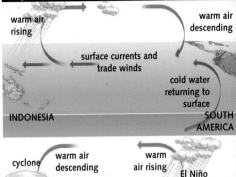

warm air rising — warm air descending
surface currents and trade winds
cold water returning to surface
INDONESIA — SOUTH AMERICA

cyclone — warm air descending — warm air rising — El Niño
surface currents and trade winds reversed — warm currents

There are numerous theories about the causes of El Niño: one of them suggests a strengthening of winds in the western Pacific; another blames an intrusion of cold air into Central Asia; and yet another considers the cause to lie in volcanic eruptions that emit ash into the atmosphere. Whatever the truth, the interaction of atmosphere and ocean figures in every theory.

Carbon in the depths of the ocean

The ocean also has an influence on the composition of the atmosphere. It absorbs about 25% of carbon emissions (some produced through human activity) by dissolving them in the surface waters and then transferring them to the ocean depths. In addition, organisms in the sea (plant plankton in particular) fix carbon as they grow.

S unshine and temperature are two of the main factors determining the climate of an area. But they are more than that: sunshine – tangible evidence of the energy supplied by the Sun – is the main force driving the circulation of the atmosphere and the ocean. It is also responsible for evaporation, the process that leads to precipitation. And the disparity between the amounts of sunshine reaching different parts of the Earth's surface is the reason for the existence of air and sea currents that tend to compensate for these unequal situations.

The Sun sends nearly all of its energy to the Earth (only a tiny part of it is devoted to its own activities, such as volcanic activity). This energy activates the circulatory system of the atmosphere.

Sunshine and temperature

Sunshine and radiation

Sunshine depends on the season, the amount of cloud and the shading effects of relief. Sunshine can also be thought of as solar radiation.

Sunshine

Sunshine (also known as 'insolation') is measured in terms of the length of time a place experiences the Sun's direct radiation. On Earth, the longest periods of sunshine are in the subtropical deserts: 3,900 hours a year in the Arizona desert and 3,600 in Egypt. The shortest periods are at high latitudes in oceanic regions (the north of Scotland, for example, with 1,050 hours a year). This disparity, where one place experiences four times as much sunshine as the other, provides a good illustration of the role played by clouds in determining hours of sunshine.

If we were to discount cloud cover and the shadows cast by areas of relief, then every place on the planet would receive the same number of hours of sunshine in the course of a year. This is known as 'maximum possible duration of sunshine' and is about 4,380 hours a year. However, these annual hours are divided up over the year in very different ways depending on latitude. At the equator, each day of the year has the same maximum theoretical duration of sunshine. At the poles, because the Earth is tilted on its axis, the annual sunshine total is distributed very unevenly, ranging from days with very long nights to days with very long periods of light. Between the equator and the poles, annual sunshine distribution varies accordingly.

The amount of sunshine in a place depends on its geographical location. In mountainous regions such as this (in the Sierra Nevada in California), the shading effect can noticeably reduce the duration of sunlight, and with it the energy that it brings. This will then in turn have an impact on relief features.

Cloud cover and relief

The discrepancy between the maximum theoretical duration of sunshine and the duration actually recorded can usually be attributed to cloud cover. The fraction of sunshine is the ratio between these two durations: for example, if the Sun has shone for half the time in a particular place, the fraction of sunshine is 50%.

Locally, sunshine can be reduced still further by shading effects. This is what often happens in mountain valleys where the high relief delays the arrival of sunshine at a particular point in the morning and brings it forward in the evening. In enclosed valleys or on north-facing slopes, this can mean a deficit of several hours of sunshine per day.

Sunny regions in particular can make good use of solar energy, but it may also be used in less obvious regions, such as those with an oceanic climate. In these cases, sunshine is seen as a complementary source of energy.

Radiation

Solar radiation represents the amount of the Sun's energy received by a surface in a day. It is expressed in kilowatt-hours per square metre (kWh/m^2). The highest figures are recorded in tropical regions. One band of radiation, where daily figures are of the order of 6–7kWh/m^2, forms an almost continuous belt along the tropic of Cancer (the deserts of Mexico and Texas, the Sahara, and deserts in the Arabian peninsula and north-east India). Another band (with radiation of the order of 5–6kWh/m^2) is to be found along the tropic of Capricorn (South America, the Namibian Desert and Australia). Between these two bands, at the equator, radiation is slightly less (4kWh/m^2). This is due to the effects of the intertropical convergence zone, in which cloud formation is extremely active. With an increase in latitude, there is a marked decrease in radiation: it drops to less then 3kWh/m^2 at around 50° in oceanic regions and at around 60° in continental regions, and to less than 2kWh/m^2 south of Greenland and around the Aleutian Islands.

Solar energy

People have always made use of the Sun's energy for drying things, whether in farming, industry or domestic life. Nowadays, thermal and photovoltaic sensors convert the photons of solar radiation into heat or electricity. This use of solar energy is being developed particularly for isolated areas, since it means that electricity can be produced in the places where it is needed without having to set up a transportation and distribution network. Thermodynamic power stations have also been developed: in these, solar energy turns water into steam which works the generators.

Map (following pages)

The length of time for which sunshine lasts is not enough on its own to describe accurately the insolation of a place: an hour of sun in summer is not the same as an hour of sun in winter, and an hour of sun at dawn is not the same as an hour of sun at midday. Therefore, insolation is also calculated in terms of energy actually received. This is expressed in kilowatt-hours (kWh) received per square metre (m^2) per day.

Solar radiation

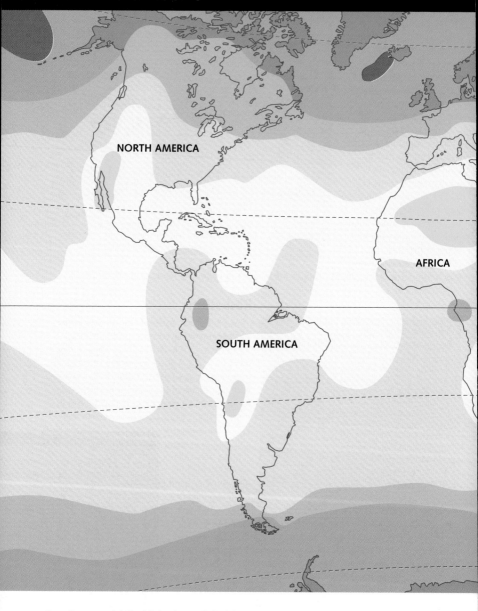

NORTH AMERICA

AFRICA

SOUTH AMERICA

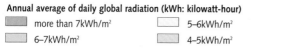

Annual average of daily global radiation (kWh: kilowatt-hour)

more than 7kWh/m²   5–6kWh/m²   3–4kWh/m²
6–7kWh/m²   4–5kWh/m²   2–3kWh/m²

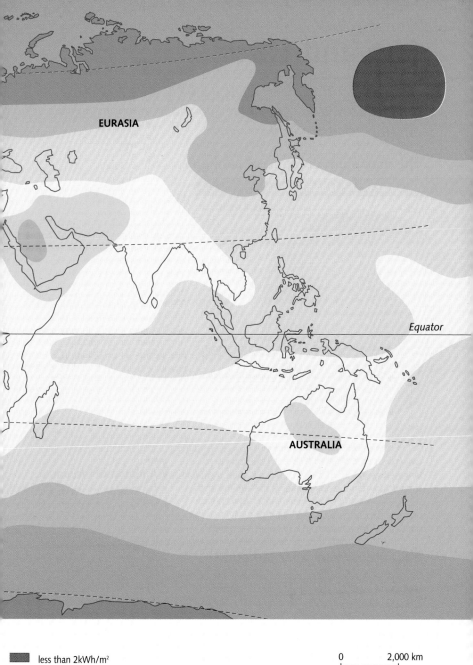

EURASIA

Equator

AUSTRALIA

less than 2kWh/m²

0   2,000 km

scale at the equator

Sun and Earth

The amount of sunshine and radiation in any one place are first and foremost a function of the Sun and its relationship with its small satellite, the Earth.

The maximum duration of sunlight

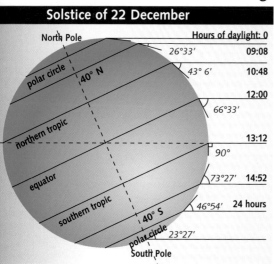

Solstice of 22 December

	Hours of daylight: 0
North Pole	
26°33'	09:08
43° 6'	10:48
40° N	12:00
polar circle	
66°33'	
northern tropic	13:12
90°	
equator	73°27' 14:52
southern tropic	46°54' 24 hours
40° S	
polar circle 23°27'	
South Pole	

The Earth rotates on its axis every 24 hours, creating the alternation of day and night.

In the course of a year, the Earth orbits the Sun, giving us the cycle of the seasons. This orbit – lasting 365 days, 6 hours and 9 minutes – is elliptical and on a plane in relation to which the Earth's axis is inclined by 23° 27'. During the course of the orbit there are some key positions, most notably the winter and summer solstices and the spring and autumn equinoxes. At midday on the summer solstice (21 or 22 June in the northern hemisphere, 22 or 23 December in the southern hemisphere), the Sun is perpendicular to the tropic of that hemisphere, which is situated at a latitude of 23° 27' from the equator. Beyond the polar circle, situated at a latitude of 23° 27' from the pole, the Sun will not set between the summer solstice and the winter solstice, which is six months later. Thus, each hemisphere has its longest day and shortest night, and its longest night and shortest day. On the other hand, at the autumn and spring equinoxes (21 September and 21 March) each point on the Earth receives 12 hours of sunlight and at midday, on the equator, the Sun passes the zenith.

The intensity of solar radiation

Latitude is a crucial factor in determining the maximum duration of sunshine and the intensity of radiation. In any one place, this intensity depends on the angle of incidence of the Sun's rays and the ability of the atmosphere to deal with them by the process called 'extinction': it reflects a proportion of them, diffuses another proportion, and absorbs another.

A matter of inclination

The word 'climate' first appeared in English in the 14th century. It came from the Late Latin *clima*, which in turn came from the Ancient Greek *klima*, meaning 'inclination', in the sense of the angle of a point on Earth relative to the Sun. This highlights the importance of the angle of the Sun's rays in relation to the Earth's surface.

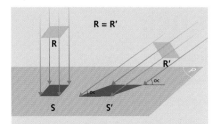

$R = R'$

S   S'

The degree of extinction of solar radiation depends on the thickness of the atmosphere through which it has to pass: the more oblique the angle of the radiation, the more it will be diffused, absorbed and reflected. Extinction depends also on the quality of the atmosphere, with air humidity, dust and pollutants all increasing the degree of extinction.

Extinction and angle of incidence often have a combined effect. At the equator, extinction is less because the atmosphere is thinner, and because the incident radiation arrives perpendicularly each time the Sun passes the zenith, which is at least once a day. Above the polar circle, only a small amount of energy is received in winter because the atmosphere is thick and the angle of incidence of the radiation becomes more and more oblique: at midday on the winter solstice it is 46° 54'.

GLOSSARY

[Angle of incidence]
Angle formed between direct radiation and the surface receiving it.

A chain of consequences

These astronomical factors influence the sunlight that we see. They are also of crucial importance with regard to other climatic features: the energy received governs temperature and evaporation as well as other weather phenomena. In particular, the Sun's energy sustains the circulation of the atmosphere and the ocean. It also explains these in so far as the transfer of masses of air or hot or cold water tends to compensate for any imbalance in the energy received from the Sun.

In Lapland, the Sun only appears for a few hours a day in winter. As it rises above the horizon, its rays shine down obliquely, lacking any real strength: the winters are therefore long and cold.

The energy balance

Every point on the Earth's surface receives a certain amount of energy and then gives back a part of it. The energy balance is the difference between the amount of energy coming in and the amount going out.

The planet's balance sheet

Taking the Earth as a whole, far and away the main source of energy coming in is from the Sun's radiation: this represents 99.98% of the total. The rest is supplied by the Earth's internal heat. Energy is lost through the atmosphere, the landmasses and the oceans. Overall, the incomings and outgoings for energy, or radiation, are equal: as much goes out as comes in. However, this energy has changed in the process: absorption, reflection and diffusion have transformed the Sun's direct radiation into diffuse, direct or thermal radiation. The balance of energy appears to be stable from one year to the next. But over the longer term this could change if, for example, the incoming energy increases or decreases as a result of developments in the Earth/Sun relationship; or if the system that operates between ocean, continent and atmosphere alters its ability to let radiation escape (due to a change in atmospheric composition or a change in reflection as a result of an alteration of the planetary albedo).

The balance of energy on the Earth's surface

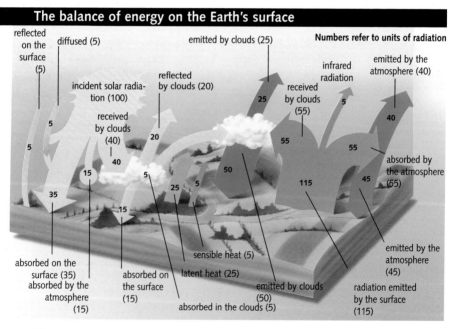

reflected on the surface (5)

diffused (5)

emitted by clouds (25)

Numbers refer to units of radiation

incident solar radiation (100)

reflected by clouds (20)

infrared radiation

emitted by the atmosphere (40)

received by clouds (40)

received by clouds (55)

5

5

35

15

20

40

5

25

5

50

55

25

55

115

45

55

40

absorbed by the atmosphere (55)

15

absorbed on the surface (35)
absorbed by the atmosphere (15)

absorbed on the surface (15)

sensible heat (5)
latent heat (25)

emitted by clouds (50)
absorbed in the clouds (5)

emitted by the atmosphere (45)

radiation emitted by the surface (115)

48

The albedo

The albedo is the ratio of reflected energy to incident energy in the wavelength of visible light. It is the albedo that makes planets 'shine': they do not supply energy themselves, but reflect part of the light that they receive from the Sun. The albedo depends on the angle of the incident radiation (the nearer the angle is to the perpendicular, the greater the reflection) and the nature of the reflecting surface. The reflective capacity of a surface depends mainly on its colour: a light-coloured surface reflects more than a dark one. Snow, for example, has an average albedo of 0.7, whereas for an evergreen forest it is 0.2. The overall

An important component in the balance of energy is the albedo, the proportion of energy that is reflected. Snow-covered ground has a higher albedo than a meadow. This is why an alteration in the albedo due to a change of land use or an increase in cloud cover can affect the local or global balance of energy.

planetary albedo is about 0.3: this means that about 30% of incoming solar energy goes out again in the form of direct radiation towards space. The albedo of landmasses is about 34%, whereas for oceans it is 26% and for clouds at low and medium altitude it is between 50% and 70%.

The balance of energy at different latitudes

Although energy is perfectly balanced on a global scale, actual places where this is the case are very few and far between. Some places receive more energy than they give out, while others give out more than they receive. Generally, there are surplus balances up as far as the latitudes between 35° and 40°. The balances then equal out, and beyond that there is a deficit. The variations in duration and area between the amount of energy received and the amount given out govern the warming and cooling of the air; this in turn contributes to the distribution of climate types and the circulation of the atmosphere and the ocean, which compensate for the effects of these variations.

The balance of energy in climate classification

Most classifications of climate are based on temperature and precipitation. However, the Russian geophysicist Mikhail Budyko is the originator of a classification based on energy distribution. Published in 1958, it built on the discovery of the laws of thermodynamics at the end of the 19th century and the progress made in instrumentation: measurements of radiation began after World War II with the invention of photocells.

Air temperature

Although primarily dependent on solar radiation, temperature is also a function of latitude. The quality of the atmosphere and the circulation of the atmosphere and the ocean also play an important role.

Composition of the atmosphere

Solar radiation is not the only factor to affect temperature: certain atmospheric gases absorb part of the solar radiation and emit it again on another wavelength, mainly infrared. The gases which have this capacity for absorption are mainly water vapour, carbon dioxide and certain gases known as 'minor gases'.

Temperature depends partly on atmospheric composition but also, more particularly, on humidity: a high level of humidity is often accompanied by thick cloud cover, which reduces the impact of sunshine. Nevertheless, assuming amounts of sunshine to be equal, it is usually less hot close to the sea than in the interior of a continent. Air density and atmospheric pressure also play a part: indeed, heat is a result of the movement and friction of gas molecules. This is why, when altitude increases and the air becomes thinner, the temperature drops.

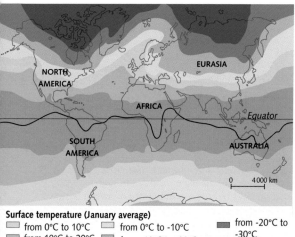

Surface temperature (January average)
- from 0°C to 10°C
- from 10°C to 20°C
- more than 20°C
- from 0°C to -10°C
- from -10°C to -20°C
- — thermal equator
- from -20°C to -30°C
- below -30°C

In January, temperature distribution at low latitudes runs parallel to the equator owing to the predominant effect of sunshine. At high latitudes in the northern hemisphere, on the other hand, the circulation of the atmosphere and the ocean, together with continentality, compensate for the weakness of the sunshine.

Circulation of the atmosphere and the ocean

The atmosphere is disturbed by strong currents that move air masses, thereby transporting large quantities of energy. As a result of atmospheric circulation, a region can be affected by an air mass with characteristics belonging to the region from which it has come. If it comes from a hot region, the air mass will be of a similar temperature and will transmit that temperature to the region to which it travels. And when two air masses with very different characteristics follow each other in quick succession – often the case in disturbances at middle latitudes – the discontinuity between the two air masses (marked by a front on the

For water to change from a liquid state to a gaseous state, the links between the water molecules have to break. This requires energy, which will be released when condensation occurs and the molecules reassemble. This stored energy is known as 'latent heat'.

weather chart) results in very abrupt changes of temperature: the air temperature suddenly plummets in the middle of the day or shoots up during the night.

The circulation of the ocean is also instrumental in transferring substantial masses of energy – witness the effect of the Gulf Stream on Europe's Atlantic coast. Sea currents like this enable coastal regions to enjoy particularly mild temperatures in relation to their latitude. On a more local level, the temperature also depends on such geographical factors as the nature of the soil, or whether there is a town, forest or lake nearby.

Spatial distribution of temperature

On a global scale, temperature distribution depends on longitude as well as latitude, since most atmospheric flows have a west-to-east component. However, it is at middle latitudes – where most mixing of air takes place – that the effect of atmospheric circulation is strongest. At high and low latitudes, near the poles and the equator, it is radiation that determines temperature.

GLOSSARY

[Hygrometry]
Measurement and study of the water vapour contained in the atmosphere.

Temperature cycles

For any one place, the average temperature is calculated for different timescales (year, month, day), but the data for maximum and minimum temperatures and for temperature range reflects the variety of situations that exist.

The importance of geographical location

Peking and Lisbon are situated at the same latitude and therefore receive, in theory, similar amounts of sunshine. But there is a great difference between the two climates. This arises from their different locations in relation to the general circulation of the atmosphere.

On an annual timescale, variations in temperature depend mainly on the supply of sunshine. Its effect is most pronounced at middle and high latitudes, where the amounts of sunshine vary most: here it is noticeably hotter in summer than in winter. However, at high and middle latitudes in winter, the most important influence is that of the atmosphere. Although there is a deficit in the balance of radiation, atmospheric gases (and in particular water vapour) act as a buffer, allowing some regions in the far north to enjoy relatively mild temperatures, particularly at a time when the circulation of the atmosphere or the ocean is bringing energy from more southerly

Measuring temperature

Temperature is extremely difficult to measure, and so strict rules need to be observed: the thermometer (or thermograph) is placed in the shade at a height of 1.5m, in a shelter with natural ventilation (usually through slits). The shelter is placed on a surface well clear of buildings, vegetation or any other obstacle (usually near an airport). These guidelines are designed to make measurements compatible with one another.

regions. For example, New York and Peking are at approximately the same latitude (40° N): the former is a coastal city, while the latter is continental. The average temperatures for July are comparable (about 25°C), while the average temperatures for January are different (1°C in New York and -6°C in Peking). In winter, humidity is the predominant influence and this favours New York. A more extreme example is Lisbon, also situated at a latitude of around 40° N, which has a slightly lower average temperature for July (20°C), but where the temperature for January is much higher (11°C). This is related to the fact that Lisbon overlooks a coast washed by western currents.

Temperature range

In general, the temperature range between summer and winter is more pronounced at high latitudes and is even greater where there is continentality: in the continental regions of Siberia and Canada, the difference can reach 40°C and even 50°C. At tropical latitudes, where there is thick cloud cover and a rainy season, maximum temperatures are reached at the end of the dry season (in spring or at the beginning of summer). In the equatorial zone, seasonal fluctuations are hardly noticeable: the temperature range between the 'hot' season and the 'cold' season is of the order of a few degrees.

Atmospheric inertia

Because of the inertia of the atmosphere, maximum and minimum temperatures are not reached until three to seven weeks after the solstice. This inertia also influences diurnal rhythms: maximum temperatures are reached several tens of minutes after the Sun has passed the zenith, and minimum temperatures occur just after sunrise.

Daytime is usually hotter than night-time, but this general rule may be broken by the advection of a particular kind of air mass: a hot air mass arriving at night or a cold air mass arriving during the day. In desert regions where atmospheric humidity does not provide a buffer, daily temperature ranges can be as much as several dozen degrees, whereas in humid regions they sometimes do not get beyond a few degrees.

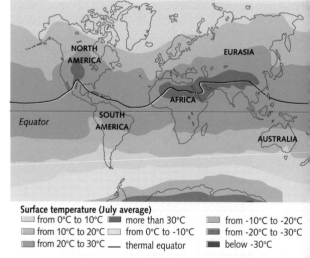

Surface temperature (July average)
- from 0°C to 10°C
- from 10°C to 20°C
- from 20°C to 30°C
- more than 30°C
- from 0°C to -10°C
- thermal equator
- from -10°C to -20°C
- from -20°C to -30°C
- below -30°C

Maximum global temperatures are reached in July, when it is summer in the northern hemisphere. The thermal equator rises to the latitude of the tropic of Cancer. In the northern hemisphere, which receives large amounts of sunlight, the isotherms are mainly parallel to the equator. The influence of the ocean is less pronounced.

The greenhouse effect

> *Some atmospheric gases act like the glass in a greenhouse: they allow the Sun's light to pass through and transform it into thermal radiation (heat) which they then retain.*

The process

The greenhouse effect is a process in which the atmosphere heats up as a result of the absorption of solar radiation by gases in the atmosphere. Part of the Sun's ultraviolet radiation is absorbed by the ozone in the stratosphere, while part of the visible light is absorbed by water vapour and aerosols. On average, half of the Sun's radiation reaches the Earth's surface, and the Earth absorbs some of it and reflects some of it. This reflection is accompanied by a change in wavelength: the reflected radiation is mainly infrared. However, the atmosphere is impervious to infrared radiation, absorbing it almost entirely. This process of absorbing (that is to say, storing) visible radiation and infrared radiation is called 'the greenhouse effect'. It is thanks to this that the average temperature on the Earth's surface is 15°C; without it, it would be -18°C. The greenhouse effect is therefore equivalent to 33°C. As well as the global greenhouse effect, there are some localized manifestations of the process: for example, on a winter's night, when the sky is cloudy, the air temperature is higher; and at the seaside, especially at night, it is milder than inland. In both cases, the cloud cover or water vapour creates a greenhouse effect by holding back the infrared radiation emitted by the Earth.

layer of gases (water vapour, carbon dioxide, methane, nitrous oxide, CFCs)

solar radiation

atmospheric pollution

infrared radiation reflected by the gases

infrared radiation reflected by the Earth

radiation absorbed by the Earth

The atmosphere and the surface of the planet absorb solar radiation and then emit it again in the form of infrared radiation, some of which is captured and stored in the form of sensible heat by greenhouse gases (water vapour, carbon dioxide, methane, etc). As a result of this process, the Earth enjoys a mild, regular mean temperature.

The gases involved

This storage process depends on the composition of the

atmosphere; not all atmospheric gases have the same ability to absorb radiation. It is mostly the minor components that have the required capability, and their presence in the air varies over time and from place to place. For example, the more humid the air and the more clouds there are, the greater the greenhouse effect and therefore the higher the temperature. Since water vapour content is closely linked to temperature, this system can maintain itself fairly easily.

Some gases are dependent on plant activity. Far from urban centres, the level of carbon dioxide fluctuates annually. In springtime in the northern hemisphere (which has a higher ratio of land to sea than the southern hemisphere), carbon dioxide content decreases as the growing season begins and photosynthesis fixes the carbon. In autumn, when photosynthetic activity slows down, the atmospheric carbon dioxide content goes up again. In the course of a year, the balance is evened out because the carbon fixed by the vegetation is restored to the atmosphere when plant remains decay.

By burning fossil fuels, which are essentially composed of carbon from the Palaeozoic era, industry and transport contribute to the amount of carbon dioxide in the atmosphere and thus increase the greenhouse effect.

The impact of human activity

Although most of these gases exist independently of human activity, some human activities do increase their concentration: one such is the burning of fossil fuels (natural gas, oil and coal) which release carbon dioxide, methane and nitrous oxide. The release of these masses of carbon can lead to local greenhouse effects in places where energy consumption is more concentrated (such as cities), or to an increased greenhouse effect over the whole planet.

Greenhouse gases				
CO_2	CH_4	N_2O	CFC-11	CFC-12
1	32	150	14 000	17 000
55 %	15 %	4 %	7 %	12 %

These figures show the radiative efficiency of certain gases, that is to say the ability of one of their molecules to absorb infrared radiation (CO_2 being used as a reference, unit: 1) and their relative contribution to an increase in the global greenhouse effect (bottom line).

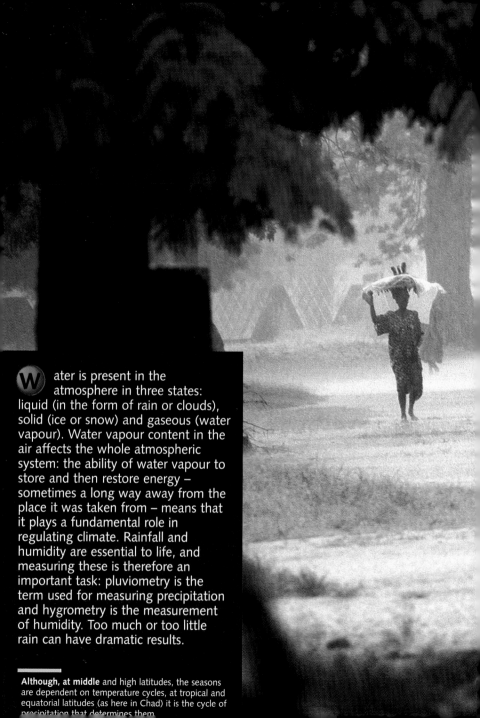

(W) ater is present in the atmosphere in three states: liquid (in the form of rain or clouds), solid (ice or snow) and gaseous (water vapour). Water vapour content in the air affects the whole atmospheric system: the ability of water vapour to store and then restore energy – sometimes a long way away from the place it was taken from – means that it plays a fundamental role in regulating climate. Rainfall and humidity are essential to life, and measuring these is therefore an important task: pluviometry is the term used for measuring precipitation and hygrometry is the measurement of humidity. Too much or too little rain can have dramatic results.

Although, at middle and high latitudes, the seasons are dependent on temperature cycles, at tropical and equatorial latitudes (as here in Chad) it is the cycle of precipitation that determines them.

Water in the atmosphere

Worldwide distribution of precipitation

Rainfall varies widely across the globe: in some places there may be a natural absence of rain for several years, in others it may rain every day, and elsewhere there may be a clearly defined rainy season.

The amount of rainfall varies widely throughout the world. In some regions, annual precipitation can be measured in tens of metres. For the populations that benefit from this, like those seen here in Indonesia, it is a godsend, although it does require careful land management.

Wide belts parallel to the equator

On a global scale, distribution of precipitation depends on where the centres of activity are located, as well as on the major atmospheric currents and the proximity of oceans and relief. There is a belt in which rain is particularly plentiful (always more than two metres a year): this is the equatorial zone, which is characterized by intertropical convergence.

At higher latitudes – about 40–50° in both hemispheres – two other high rainfall bands are linked to the westerly winds and the disturbances they bring with them. Between these two bands and the equatorial belt, at latitudes of about 20–30°, there are two other symmetrical zones of low rainfall: these are linked to subtropical high pressure. The latitudes near to the poles are also arid zones and the high pressure found here makes it harder for humid air to rise and for it to move horizontally (known as advection).

Proximity to oceans and continentality

On top of this latitudinal distribution there is an asymmetry between east and west: at low latitudes the eastern sides are wetter than the western sides because of the trade winds. These are moist winds that blow from the north-east to the south-west in the northern hemisphere, and from the south-east to the north-west in the southern hemisphere. At middle latitudes, because of the westerly winds, the opposite happens, and it is the western sides of continents that are wetter. In both cases, rainfall gradually diminishes as the

Some deserts (such as in Nevada in the USA, seen here) do not get rain every year. This may exclude the possibility of people settling in such areas, since water is essential to life.

Measuring precipitation

The level of rainfall is measured with a pluviometer (or rain gauge) for manual readings, or a pluviograph for automatic readings. The edge of the receptacle must be located at a height of 1.5m on a piece of open ground. A millimetre of collected water is equivalent to a volume of 1 litre per m².

air moves further inland and loses its moisture. Finally, mountains – in particular the Rockies, the Andes and the Himalayas – act as (often insurmountable) barriers to humid winds. This explains why the exposed sides of mountains, facing the humid air flows, are wetter than the sheltered sides, where pockets of aridity sometimes develop. Conversely, large interior lakes like the American Great Lakes or the Caspian Sea can help to replenish the air flows with water.

The hot season and the humid season

Within each general rainfall pattern, there is a great deal of variation. The equatorial band is characterized by precipitation that is uniformly distributed through the year. Further from the equator, the tropical regions experience one or two rainy seasons quite near to the summer solstice. The rainy season is shorter the higher the latitude. At middle and high latitudes, precipitation is greater in summer than in winter, because the summer heat increases evaporation and cloud formation. The only type of climate for which the hot season is not the humid season is the Mediterranean climate.

Map (following pages)

World distribution of rainfall is dependent on the distribution of temperature (which affects the ability of air to evaporate), the distribution of centres of activity (which govern the processes leading to the formation of precipitation), the distribution of oceans over which air masses become charged with water vapour, and the distribution of relief features which trigger the release of precipitation.

Annual precipitation

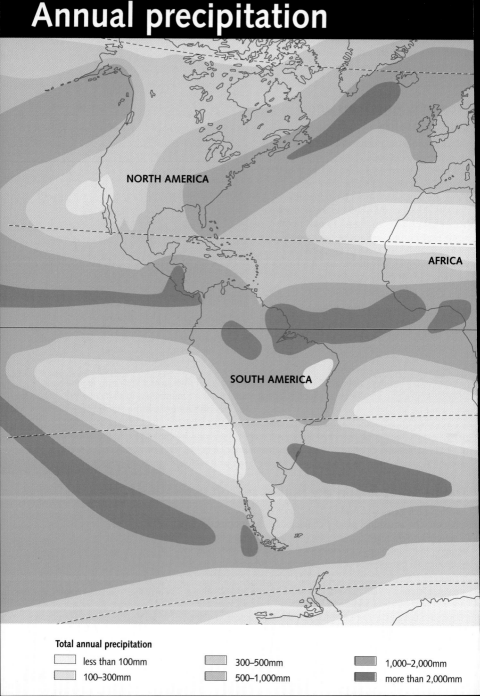

NORTH AMERICA

AFRICA

SOUTH AMERICA

Total annual precipitation

- less than 100mm
- 100–300mm
- 300–500mm
- 500–1,000mm
- 1,000–2,000mm
- more than 2,000mm

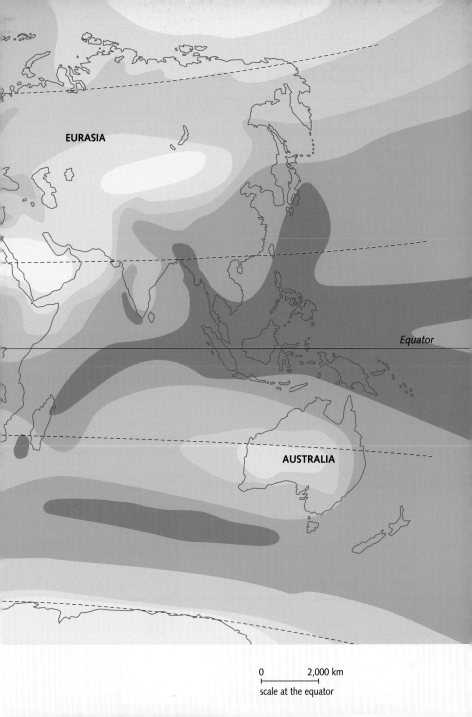

EURASIA

Equator

AUSTRALIA

0   2,000 km

scale at the equator

Hygrometry

Hygrometry is the measurement of the water vapour contained in the air (humidity), which varies according to temperature and pressure. Precipitation can only begin to form when the air is saturated with water vapour.

Water vapour in the atmosphere

In the lower atmosphere, below 6km, air always contains water vapour: the water contained in this layer represents 90% of the water in the atmosphere. Even in regions badly affected by drought, relative humidity below 20% is rare, while in temperate regions 90% relative humidity is reached almost every day. Generally, air is considered dry if it has a relative humidity of below 35%, and humid if it has a relative humidity of above 70%.

What influences humidity

Relative humidity is the most common measurement used to describe the amount of water in the air: the water mass contained in a particular volume of air is expressed as a ratio of the maximum mass that this volume of air can contain at a given temperature and pressure. This value provides the best

Weather satellites carry out measurements of water vapour, which absorbs the signal given out by the satellite. In a picture of this type, the surface of the globe becomes invisible: only the vortices corresponding to centres of activity, jet streams and cloud tops are apparent.

indication of how close the air is to being saturated with water – this is the point at which condensation (passing into a liquid state) and precipitation (the falling of this liquid water) may be triggered. The mass of water vapour that a volume of air can contain increases with temperature; the temperature at which saturation is reached is called 'dew-point temperature'. Atmospheric pressure also affects air humidity:

Hair as an instrument

The hygrometer is the most common instrument for measuring air humidity, and the hair hygrometer dates back to 1783. It is based on the fact that a hair changes its length in accordance with the ambient humidity, becoming shorter when the atmosphere is dry and lengthening when the air is humid. The hair hygrometer is considered to be very reliable, at least for relative humidity values above 20%.

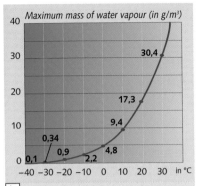

Maximum mass of water vapour (in g/m³)

- 40
- 30 — 30,4
- 20 — 17,3
- 10 — 9,4
- 0,34
- 0,9 — 4,8
- 0,1 — 2,2

−40 −30 −20 −10 0 10 20 30 in °C

The capacity of air to contain water vapour increases rapidly with temperature: the warmer it is, the more can contain.

when pressure increases, the air contracts while the water mass contained in it remains unchanged. So, humidity increases relative to the volume of air, which has decreased. Conversely, when atmospheric pressure decreases, air expands, the water is dispersed throughout a greater volume, and the relative humidity goes down. These two processes – change of temperature and change of pressure – play an important part in condensation, and therefore in the formation of precipitation.

Humidity distribution

On a global scale, humidity distribution corresponds more or less to temperature distribution. Humidity decreases from the equator towards the poles. Proximity to a water supply also plays a role: humidity decreases as oceans get further away and as continentality increases. Atmospheric circulation compensates for these decreases (whether connected with latitude or continentality) by bringing in humid air masses. Humidity in the atmosphere is very sensitive to local factors such as the presence of a lake, a marsh or a forest; and a bare rocky surface can change the water content of the air quite radically. Because of the importance of pressure and temperature, humidity is also closely related to altitude. In the course of a year, relative humidity always develops according to temperature and atmospheric circulation. In the course of a day, unless there is some meteorological incident, it follows the temperature rhythm: maximum humidity is reached at the end of the night and minimum humidity at the beginning of the afternoon.

One of the distinctive features of the Earth is that it contains water in all its forms – liquid, solid and gaseous – as illustrated by this satellite view of Lake Geneva, with alpine glaciers and clouds. However, there is no visible sign of water vapour despite the fact that this gas is present on every part of the Earth's surface – even in the most arid deserts, where the air is never completely dry.

The water cycle

*Water is constantly moving around on the Earth, changing
from a liquid state to a gaseous or solid state. These
movements and changes of state are together known as
the 'water cycle' or 'hydrological cycle'.*

Water on Earth: different types of reservoir

The amount of water on the Earth is estimated to be 1,370 million km³, which is distributed
in various reservoirs. Of these, the ocean is the most important, with 97% of the total of the
Earth's water. Two per cent is frozen in glaciers and the remaining 1% is contained in
groundwater, lakes, soil water, rivers and living organisms. The atmosphere contains less than
0.001% of the Earth's total water. Despite this relatively small quantity, the atmosphere has a
special role to play: water vapour is circulated by means of atmospheric currents and can

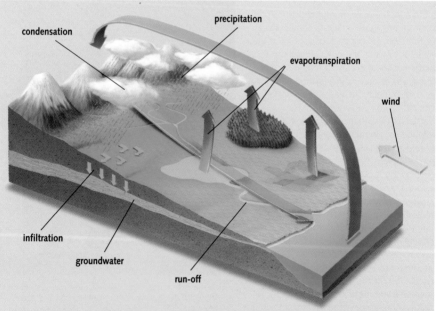

condensation

precipitation

evapotranspiration

wind

infiltration

groundwater

run-off

The atmospheric part of the water cycle – in other words, the annual amount of water that
evaporates and produces rain – is estimated at 496,000km³. Evaporation is thought to be
423,100km³ at sea, as against 72,900km³ on land. Precipitation is thought to be 385,700km³
at sea and 110,300km³ on land.

GLOSSARY

[Evaporation]
Transformation of water
from a liquid state to a
gaseous state.

sometimes condense far away from the place where it was formed. Water vapour thus creates a link between geographical places and reservoirs that are a great distance from each other. It is estimated that the average time for a water molecule to remain in a given place in the atmosphere before moving to another reservoir is about ten days, as against 37,000 years in the ocean. Thus, even if the volume of water recycled is small, the instability of the atmospheric system means that large quantities of water eventually change place.

The atmosphere and other reservoirs

The part of the water cycle concerning the atmosphere is mainly the link between the ocean and continents. Sea water is transferred to the atmosphere through evaporation, is then restored to continents through precipitation, and eventually returns to the ocean through run-off in rivers. On this general basis, there are direct transfers between the atmosphere on the one hand and lakes, rivers and vegetation on the other. If the Earth's stock of water and that of each of the reservoirs are considered to be stable, the quantity of water that evaporates each year, taken as a whole, is equal to the quantity of water that falls as precipitation. For oceans, there is more evaporation than precipitation, whereas the reverse is true for continents. Run-off balances things out, allowing the water received on continents to drain away towards the oceans and enabling oceans to regain the water they have lost through evaporation.

The amount of water contained in the atmosphere is considered to be stable, insofar as the temperature of the Earth's atmosphere is stable too: an increase in temperature would cause an increase in evaporation and thus in precipitation.

Water is also transferred in space, on a global scale: in the equatorial zone and at middle latitudes, the gains through precipitation are greater than the losses through evaporation; at low and very high latitudes, on the other hand, the losses are greater than the gains.

The seas and oceans contain 97% of the Earth's water and occupy almost two thirds of its surface: they play a fundamental role in the water cycle, in exchanges of energy and in the functioning of the atmosphere.

Not only water ...

The transfer of water from oceans to continents is accompanied by substantial transfers of energy: in order to separate water molecules from each other, evaporation requires a certain amount of energy which is 'stored' by water vapour in the form of latent heat. When condensation takes place, this energy is released in the form of sensible heat. It is estimated that 45% of the energy absorbed by continents and oceans is for the purpose of evaporation. Water vapour thus plays a fundamental role in regulating the Earth's energy.

Clouds and cloud cover

Formed from minute water droplets and/or ice crystals
suspended in the atmosphere, clouds (and precipitation) are
the most tangible evidence of water in the atmosphere.

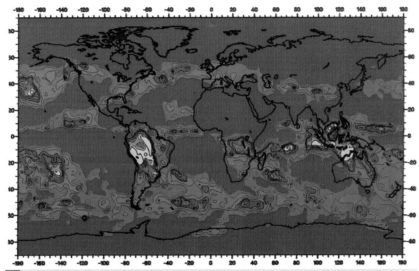

Satellites have transformed the study of cloud cover, enabling observations to be made of entire cloud systems. The use of sensors to measure visible and infrared radiation provides very clear details of the largest clouds, called cumulonimbuses, which can be as tall as 18km in the tropical zone.

Observing cloud cover

Cloud cover in a particular location is measured first and foremost as the length of time when clouds prevent direct radiation in relation to the number of hours during which the Sun could have shone. It is the inverse of what is known as the fraction of sunshine. On a global scale, cloud cover rarely exceeds 90% and it can go down to 25%. But all that this period of cloud cover tells us is that clouds

Types of clouds

Since 1896, clouds have been classified into ten major types based on their appearance: cirrus, cirrocumulus, cirrostratus, altocumulus, altostratus, nimbostratus, stratocumulus, stratus, cumulus and cumulonimbus. Further subdivision distinguishes between those arranged in strata, those in the form of fish-scales (mackerel sky) and so on. Particular features such as mammas (protuberances) or tubas (cones like an upside-down funnel) can then be identified. Of the ten cloud types listed, only six are likely to produce rain.

are present between the Sun and the observer.

Further observations are required: certain clouds are studied in detail, especially those, such as cirrus clouds, which do not mask direct solar radiation. The spatial extent of cloud cover is expressed as the proportion of sky occupied by cloud.

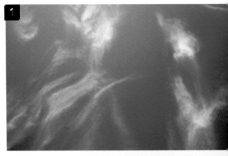

Cloud formation

Almost all clouds are formed in the troposphere (below 10km in altitude), where water vapour is concentrated. They form when the air becomes saturated with water vapour, which then condenses into tiny droplets. Usually, air reaches saturation point by cooling – this can occur due to advection over a cold surface (for example, when a mass of moist sea air arrives over a continent which has cooled down) – by orographic ascent (over rising ground) or dynamic ascent (convection), or within a disturbance (when a mass of warm humid air 'traps' a colder air mass). The tiny droplets are about 0.02mm in diameter on average (ranging from 0.008mm to 0.8mm), the exact size varying from one cloud to another and also within the same cloud. Below 0°C, they can freeze into ice crystals. A cloud breaks up because of precipitation, but more often because the tiny droplets evaporate when the air warms up.

> **GLOSSARY**
>
> **[Advection]**
> Horizontal movement of an air mass.
> **[Convection]**
> Transfer of heat in a fluid through the movement of molecules from a cooler, more dense region to a warmer, less dense region.

The global distribution of cloud cover

The cloudiest regions in the world are those with the greatest humidity and in which the ascent of air necessary to cloud formation is an active feature. These regions are the equatorial zone (dynamic ascent), oceanic regions (disturbances and advections of humid air) and mountainous regions (orographic ascent). Apart from in regions characterized by advections of humid air, the most favourable season for cloud formation is summer, when evaporation and convection are more intense because of high temperatures and warming of the Earth's surface.

Three sorts of cloud (from top to bottom): cirrus (composed of ice crystals), cirrocumulus (which does not produce precipitation) and cumulonimbus (a very tall cloud, in which the largest raindrops form).

How precipitation forms

Precipitation is water in liquid or solid form that falls to the ground. The air needs to become saturated with water before the water can condense.

Saturation

The first stage in precipitation is saturation. The quantity of water vapour must reach or even exceed the maximum that can be sustained at a given temperature or pressure. In other words, the level of relative humidity needs to reach 100%.

The level of relative humidity depends not only on the quantity of water but also on the temperature and pressure of the particular volume of air. Only one of these variables needs to change in order for saturation point to be reached. This might happen, for example, when air is enriched with water vapour by flowing over a mass of water in an ocean, sea or lake; or when it cools upon contact with a cold surface (as when a mass of sea air reaches a continent that has cooled down in winter); or when, on

cold front   warm front

meeting of air masses

orographic   dynamic

Ascent is a basic process in cloud formation and in triggering precipitation. Different types of ascent are shown above.

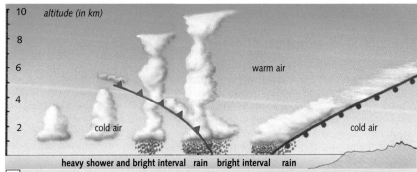

10   *altitude (in km)*

8

6   warm air

4

2   cold air   cold air

heavy shower and bright interval   rain   bright interval   rain

The cloud system linked to a cyclonic disturbance is made up of an advance band of cirrus clouds, a band (corresponding to the warm front) formed by altostratus, nimbus and nimbostratus clouds, and a back edge (corresponding to the cold front) formed by cumulus clouds.

reaching a higher altitude, it encounters rising ground; or when a lighter hot air mass catches up with a cold air mass and rides up over it; or when moist air is subject to convection; or, finally, when at high altitude an advection of cold air occurs.

Condensation

Once saturation point is reached, the water vapour condenses and passes from a gaseous state to a liquid or solid state. In order to do this, the water vapour adheres around tiny solid particles (possibly volcanic ash, sea salt or dust) known as 'condensation nuclei', whose size is roughly 0.1 micrometre (a micrometre is one millionth of a metre).

A cloud made up of tiny droplets or crystals appears. Then, inside it, various contradictory processes take place: condensation is accompanied by a release of latent heat, and therefore an increase in sensible heat, which limits the condensation. At the same time, the warming of the air encourages evaporation, and therefore a return to saturation and condensation. In short, a water molecule may pass from a liquid state to a gaseous state several times before falling.

Precipitation

The tiny droplets or ice crystals are at first too light to fall, but by colliding and gradually amalgamating (a process known as agglomeration), they eventually reach a critical weight and fall as precipitation. The critical weight

 The methods may have changed, but this picture from 1910 shows that man has striven for many years to be master of the climate. This desire is as strong now as it ever was.

Triggering precipitation

Techniques for preventing hail, triggering rain or eliminating fog mostly concist of scattering condensation nuclei such as salt particles into a cloud. Apart from pollution problems, these techniques create political difficulties: the region that benefits from the precipitation does so at the expense of the region that should have received it.

depends on the ascending currents within the cloud. In fact, if the evaporation and ascending processes are added together, only 10% of the water contained in clouds reaches the ground.

The agglomeration of the droplets depends on the prevailing conditions within the cloud. When the temperature is below 0°C, the droplets freeze and the water agglomerates (the 'cold wall effect'). If there is strong turbulence inside the cloud, the fastest-moving drops pick up the slowest ones (coalescence). The more instability there is, the more coalescence there is and the larger the drops. This is what happens in cumulonimbus clouds, which build to great heights and in which there are powerful ascending currents. After several return journeys between the bottom and top of the cloud, the droplet, sometimes of a considerable size, finally falls to the ground.

Water in the atmosphere **69**

Rain, drizzle, snow ...

Precipitation includes a wide variety of what are called 'hydrometeors': rain, drizzle, snow and hail. The size of the particles varies between 0.2mm and several centimetres.

Liquid hydrometeors

Drizzle is made up of very small hydrometeors measuring between 0.2mm and 0.5mm. These fall very slowly, with the droplets seeming to float in the air. They are formed in stratus clouds at low altitude, and internal movement is very restricted, which limits coalescence.

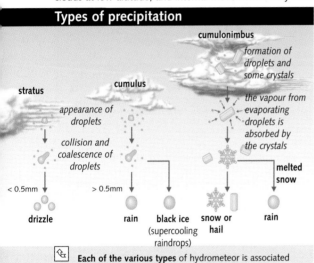

Types of precipitation

cumulonimbus

formation of droplets and some crystals

cumulus

the vapour from evaporating droplets is absorbed by the crystals

stratus

appearance of droplets

collision and coalescence of droplets

melted snow

< 0.5mm   > 0.5mm

drizzle   rain   black ice   snow or   rain
                          (supercooling hail
                          raindrops)

Each of the various types of hydrometeor is associated with a specific cloud type.

The intensity of drizzle is so low that rain gauges cannot detect it: weather stations record it simply as a trace, which at least indicates that precipitation has occurred, even if it has not produced much water.

Rain is the name given to precipitation when the drops are between 0.5mm and 6mm in diameter. The speed at which the drops fall depends on their size: the largest drops can reach more than 30kph. Rain is recorded by the depth of water collected (in millimetres), and if possible the duration of the period of rain is specified. Pluviograms are used to show intensity.

Solid hydrometeors

Hail falls in the form of hailstones: hydrometeors made of ice, whose size varies between 5mm and 50mm, sometimes more. Smaller particles, known as fine hail, are made up of agglomerated crystals of snow and ice which are white and flaky and between 1mm and 5mm in diameter. They usually form under supercooling conditions: this is when water in the atmosphere remains liquid although the air temperature is below freezing point. This happens especially in cumulonimbus clouds, where water vapour first condenses into ice nuclei, around which water agglomerates through a cold wall effect. As hailstones travel back and forth between the bottom and top of the cloud, they become bigger before finally falling to the ground. Sometimes hailstones melt as they travel through the warm layers of

On average, snow is thought to be ten times less dense than water: 10mm of snow is therefore equivalent to 1mm of rain, although the actual equivalence depends on the actual density of the snow. In climatology, snow level is always expressed as an equivalent water level. It is measured using a pluviometer, or rain gauge, fitted with a heating element.

the lower atmosphere, and then they fall to the ground as drops of water. Hail and fine hail are measured in the same way as rain, by the depth of melted water. Snow crystals in branch or star form develop when the temperature of the cloud is below freezing: ice crystals develop around the condensation nuclei and agglomerate due to the cold wall effect or by colliding with one another. The most beautiful crystals and the largest flakes are formed in clouds with low turbulence. Snow is measured using a snow gauge, which is a rain gauge fitted with a heating element to make the snow melt.

Some particular phenomena

In tropical maritime regions, it can rain in summer without there being any clouds. Known as 'serein', this rain consists of very large condensation nuclei which quickly form into large drops, although they are relatively small in number. Sometimes a rainbow is the only visible evidence of this precipitation.

When condensation occurs directly on the ground in temperate regions, dew forms. This happens at the end of the night when it is not very cloudy and when the ground has cooled down. If the temperature is below freezing point, the dew turns into hoarfrost. Black ice is supercooled rain that has fallen onto a frozen surface. Freezing fog is a dense fog that condenses into ice if it comes into contact with cold surfaces.

GLOSSARY

[Coalescence]
Process by which tiny droplets grow in size by colliding with one another.

Storms

Storms are atmospheric phenomena involving a cumulonimbus cloud, thunder, lightning and often heavy precipitation.

How storms form

Each year there are 40 million storms on the Earth, which works out at about 110,000 storms each day. Storms are most frequent at low latitudes, where it is common for cumulonimbus clouds to develop. They are also frequent in summer at middle latitudes, when convection is strong. For the same reasons, there are more storms on continents than at sea. However, if convective air masses move, then storms can occur at any season in any region.

A storm cloud develops when a strong ascent occurs within an air mass. The air rises, then cools, and condensation begins. This condensation causes a release of latent heat, which warms the surrounding air; since warm air is lighter than cold air, it continues to rise. When this process is particularly active, the cumulonimbus has an anvil-shaped top and may be up to 25km in diameter and between 13km (at middle latitudes) and 18km tall (at low latitudes). These rapid ascents of air occur when the vertical thermal gradient is strong: for example, when two air masses with contrasting temperatures come into contact, when there is a horizontal movement of cold air at high altitude, or when the ground has heated up a lot (storms are then often triggered at the end of the day, and die down during the night).

GLOSSARY

[Thermal gradient] Rate of temperature variation on a horizontal or vertical plane.

Characterized by strong vertical movements, a storm cloud contains negative ions at its base and positive ions in its central and upper parts. Contact between these opposite charges triggers lightning.

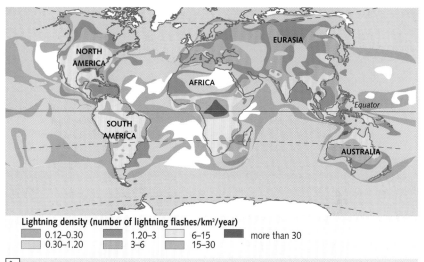

Lightning density (number of lightning flashes/km²/year)
- 0.12–0.30
- 0.30–1.20
- 1.20–3
- 3–6
- 6–15
- 15–30
- more than 30

Observation of lightning is carried out by satellites and radar. The information obtained is processed in real time and the progress of storm clouds can thus be monitored.

Wind, rain, thunder and lightning

A storm can last anything from several minutes to several hours, depending on the degree of convection. It is accompanied by gusts of wind and, very often, by heavy showers of rain or hail. The raindrops or hailstones are often very large because the instability within the cloud encourages them to increase in size through coalescence or a cold wall effect.

A storm is accompanied by thunder and lightning. The lightning is an electrical discharge triggered by opposite charges within a cloud, or between two clouds, or between the cloud and the ground. Although it only lasts a few tenths of a second, lightning causes heat to be released, which often increases the temperature of the surrounding air to over 20,000°C. The subsequent increase in pressure generates an acoustic shock wave, which we hear as thunder.

The light from the lightning flash spreads at a speed of 300,000km/s and the noise from the thunder at 0.330km/s (330m/s). This is why, unless the storm is directly overhead, there is a fairly long interval between seeing the flash and hearing the thunder, and the length of this delay enables us to calculate how far away the storm is. Lightning can be visible up to 100km away, while thunder is audible only up to 20km away.

Other lights in the sky

The atmosphere contains other bright lights, all indicating the presence of condensed water. Two luminous circles sometimes appear to surround the Sun and the Moon in the form of a halo and a ring. The halo is white or iridescent, while the ring is smaller and made up of bands of colour. In both, the light has been broken up by ice crystals or ice-crystal clouds. A rainbow is a group of concentric arcs in all the colours of the spectrum. It occurs when light is refracted and reflected by a screen of water droplets.

Although human beings can live in almost any sort of climate, some climates are more favourable than others. The most heavily populated regions of the world all have warm temperate climates. As well as providing good living conditions, these regions have plant life which is active enough to support animals and humans. In such climates, neither temperature, humidity or rainfall are limiting factors, even if plants, animals and humans have had to adapt to their particular features: hot and cold seasons, or dry and rainy seasons.

Rainy seasons, dry seasons, hot summers, hard winters, mild damp weather – whatever their particular characteristics, most climates have allowed life to develop, and plant and animal species have adapted accordingly.

Climates that support life

Temperate climate – moderate climate?

> We think of a temperate climate as being a moderate climate, without extremes. However, every type of climate has its extreme moments.

Averages and extremes

The description and study of climate is based on statistical calculations made using data collected by weather stations. The main parameters studied are wind speed and direction, sunshine and cloud cover, temperatures and air humidity (precipitation and other forms of water in the atmosphere). These measurements are made under strict conditions over long periods of time and at regular intervals: once a day for precipitation, two to eight times a day for temperature, and continuously for wind. This allows averages to be calculated for a range of timescales (weeks, months, years, decades). A 30-year period is often used as a basis, and references to this are known as 'mean'. So, for example, the maximum normal temperature in London for the month of July will be the average daily maximum temperatures recorded each July over a period of 30 years. However, averages can mislead us into thinking that the climate is fixed, and can obscure extreme values. This is why climatology is interested in amplitude – the gap between maximum and minimum values – which introduces the idea of variability.

Climatologists are also interested in record values: even if these do not necessarily have any statistical meaning, they at least provide some idea of the limits of the atmospheric system.

Wind and rain

Record values for temperature and sunshine are found at very high latitudes and in tropical deserts, but record values for other parameters have been documented at middle or low latitudes, in climatic zones that more readily support life.

Tornadoes are one example. Although impossible to measure accurately because of their erratic and destructive force, they are thought to reach 500kph. Actual maximums of 371kph

Each year, the Indian monsoon is accompanied by torrential rain. This climate holds the record for annual precipitation, and yet a whole continent has adapted to it.

(Mount Washington, USA, 1934) and 320kph (Mount Ventoux, southern France, 1967) have been measured.

The Himalayas hold the record for precipitation with an annual total of 11m at Cherrapunji, compared with 0.60m each year in London. These are annual averages – the absolute record is 26m between 1 August 1860 and 31 July 1861. Record values for rainfall intensity are achieved during storms (in the Mediterranean region, for example). However, the record for the number of days with storms is held by Java in Indonesia: 322 days during 1916. The heaviest hailstone, weighing 1.9kg, was recovered in Kazakhstan in 1959. And the heaviest snowfalls have been in the USA: 31m in one year

After an ice storm in the USA. Even apparently mild climates can experience catastrophic weather events that devastate both the natural world and human activity.

(1971–2) at Paradise in Washington State, and 1.93m in 24 hours at Silver Lake in Colorado. Records for drought are, of course, to be found in deserts: Egypt went for ten years with an annual rainfall average of only 2mm, and without a drop of rain at all for many years.

Hot and sunny, cold and dark

Record sunshine has been recorded in the Sahara (97%) and in Arizona (91%). Minimum amounts are to be found at the South and North Poles, with 182 and 176 sunless days respectively. Records for temperature follow the same pattern: the highest temperature (58°) was recorded in Libya in 1922 and the lowest (-89°) in Antarctica in 1983. The greatest amplitude is found at Verkhoïansk in Siberia, which holds the record for the biggest difference between minimum and maximum temperatures in a year: 104°C.

Map *(following pages)*

Temperature is one of the main criteria for classifying climate. Another is humidity: precipitation and other forms of water in the atmosphere. These two parameters have the strongest influence on biological activity. However, there is a great deal of variation between the different climates – continental, oceanic, equatorial and subtropical – as regards temperature, rainfall and seasons.

NORTH AMERICA

AFRICA

SOUTH AMERICA

Continental cold temperate climate

Extreme continental cold temperate climate

Temperate transitional oceanic climate

Temperate oceanic climate

Limit of average temperatures below 10°C for the hottest month

Maritime zones with low precipitation (below 500mm)

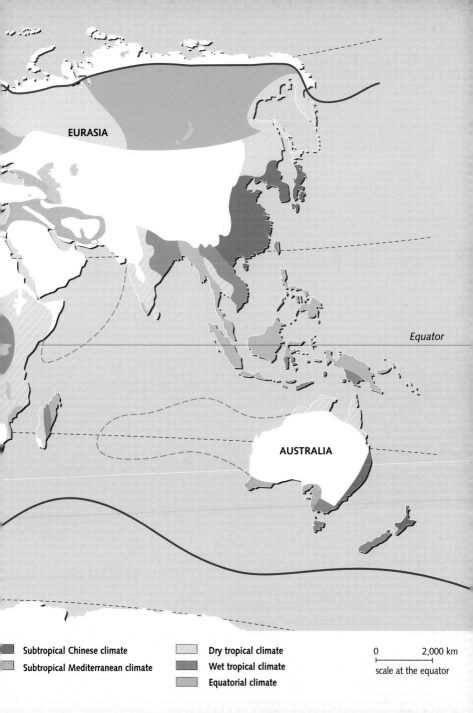

EURASIA

Equator

AUSTRALIA

■ Subtropical Chinese climate   Dry tropical climate   0   2,000 km

■ Subtropical Mediterranean climate   ■ Wet tropical climate   scale at the equator

□ Equatorial climate

The temperate oceanic climate

Significant features of the temperate oceanic climate are winds and a lack of contrast between rainfall and temperature in the different seasons (winters tend to be mild, and summers on the cool side).

On the western coasts of continents

An oceanic climate is found at middle latitudes, between 35° and 60°, on the western coasts of continental landmasses: the coastal strip of the American continent bordering the Pacific, bounded by the Rockies and the Andes; the small southern tip of Australia; Tasmania and New Zealand; and Europe. This type of climate is most extensive in Europe, because of the absence of mountain barriers running from north to south: it covers an area stretching from the coasts of Scandinavia and northern Spain as far east as the Black Sea and the plains of southern Russia. Here it develops its most subtle variations, as it gradually changes from being hyperoceanic (or 'true oceanic') over the British Isles to being more continental (or 'transitional oceanic') on the plains of central and eastern Europe – the oceanic influence becomes weaker as one goes further into the continental landmass.

Constant humidity and moderate temperatures tend to encourage plant growth. However, most species have a dormant period during the winter, since plant rhythms are affected by the number of hours of daylight.

Moderate temperatures

In a 'true oceanic' climate, the winters are mild and the summers cool; frost and heat waves are exceptional, and the annual temperature range is between 5°C and 12°C. Winds are strong and frequent, sometimes turning into gales that can be very destructive. The air is humid all through the year and cloud cover is thick, thereby reducing the amount of sunshine. Precipitation is greater in the north than in the south of this climatic area, with average precipitation levels on the plains varying between 600mm and 2,200mm a year. The cool season is generally showery, and there is rarely a day, let alone a month, without some form of precipitation. This generally takes the form of drizzle or showers which can last for hours, although one of the main features of the oceanic climate is the speed with which precipitation alternates with sunny spells, or calm periods with gusty winds. All of these characteristics become weaker as continentality increases: the seasons are better defined, the temperature range is greater and the winds are less strong.

Wind can be a limiting factor in plant development because of its physical force. The deformed shapes of some trees (as seen here in the Irish countryside) bear witness to this.

Westerly winds

The oceanic climate is found in regions where westerly winds and the high-altitude polar jet stream feature strongly. It is here that polar and tropical air masses confront one another. In winter, the contrast between polar and tropical air is very strong, and there are very active disturbances in addition to thick cloud cover. Over the north and east of the area, invasions of the cold anticyclone can produce cold dry bright days. In summer, on the other hand, the disturbance in the air flow is less significant because the contrast in temperature between the two air masses is less marked. Winds are weaker and less regular. In addition, the tropical anticyclonic belt (as around the Azores in Europe, California in North America, and Easter Island off South America) may occasionally move to higher latitudes, creating dry sunny warm periods, especially at lower latitudes. Only the middle latitudes (Great Britain, for example) are sometimes subject to disturbed air currents all year round.

Climates that support life

The continental climate

The continental climate is characterized by hard winters and mild or hot summers which are relatively rainy. There are slight variations to this, as with most climate types.

Only in the northern hemisphere

The continental climate has very distinct seasons, with hard winters and hot summers. The transitional seasons, on the other hand, are short and spectacular: within the space of a few days in autumn, the trees produce a vibrant display of colours as the leaves fall in preparation for winter.

The continental climate (or cold temperate climate) is found at middle and high latitudes in the northern hemisphere. There are no continental landmasses at similar latitudes in the southern hemisphere, and consequently no continental climate there either. It ranges over the northern part of America and Eurasia. In Europe, it covers the interior of Scandinavia and continental Russia as far as the Urals. Beyond the Urals, an extreme continental climate is found. We then find the continental climate again in the north of China and along the Siberian coast as far as Kamchatka. In North America, it extends from Alaska to Canada and the Great Lakes.

Temperature range and precipitation

Cold sharp winters, hot summers, short springs and autumns with dazzling colours, are typical of the continental climate – it is notable for its broad annual temperature range. For three to four months, the average temperature drops below freezing point, often going down to -30°C or -40°C for short or long periods. Between June and August, the average temperature reaches 20°C or higher. The temperature range between the coldest month and the hottest month is practically double that of oceanic regions: for example, Moscow has a range of 29°C, as against 18°C in Copenhagen, situated at the same latitude.

Precipitation is quite low because of the distance from the sea and the weakness or absence of air flows from the west. However, rainfall is rarely a limiting factor because low levels occur in winter when the vegetation has little need of water; in summer, rain is relatively abundant, due to significant amounts of convection.

Winter is a time when plant growth is severely restricted. For several months, the rhythm of plant life is slowed down by the cold and the snow.

High pressure in winter, convection in summer

Because of the high-latitude location, solar radiation is not very effective in winter, and high-pressure areas of thermal origin set in. These anticyclones prevent the humid western currents from penetrating inland – the currents have, in any case, slipped further south at this time of the year. Nevertheless, they sometimes manage to get through, bringing some precipitation in the form of snow, which covers the ground until the spring thaw; the snow cover then reinforces the thermal high pressure. Only the eastern edges of the climatic area, such as Quebec or the eastern coast of the USA, receive plentiful winter precipitation because of sea air penetrating from the east. This then produces snowstorms which can last several days, with much thicker snow cover than in more westerly regions. During the summer, solar radiation is greater because of the longer day. Thus, convection develops and air masses become more humid because of the moisture evaporating from the water-soaked ground. The masses of sea air brought in by the westerly winds are also made unstable by convection. This is the stormy season.

Imprecise boundaries

In Europe, the boundary between continental climate and oceanic climate is difficult to define because of the absence of mountain barriers that would mark a clear transition. This highlights how different climatic criteria are used to define different types of climate: thus, north-west Russia is considered to have a continental climate if the focus is on winter temperatures, as is northern Italy if the focus is on precipitation.

Climates that support life **83**

The subtropical climate

Cool or mild, rainy in winter, hot in summer – the subtropical climate has a very high annual temperature range and two summer rainfall patterns.

The climates of the subtropical margins

The subtropical climate covers two climate types – the Mediterranean climate and the Chinese climate – found between the middle latitudes and the tropical zone. Linked to westerly air currents, the Mediterranean climate is found on the western sides of continents at a latitude of between 30° and 45°, where it adjoins the temperate oceanic climate: it is found in the Mediterranean Basin as far east as Iran, in California, in Chile, in south-western South Africa and in south-western Australia. Its counterpart is the Chinese climate, which is slightly lower in latitude (25–35°) and found on the eastern sides of continents, covering a large area of the south-eastern USA, China and Japan, southern Brazil, south-eastern South Africa, eastern Australia and northern New Zealand. The Mediterranean and Chinese climates form a transitional area between the temperate zone and the hot zone. Because of their transitional location, there can be marked

In Europe, olive trees are fairly good indicators of the boundaries of the Mediterranean climate. This shows how, in some cases, the extent of a climate can be defined by plant formations (open savanna grasslands, coniferous forests, and so on) or by particular species. For example, a feature of the olive tree is that it cannot sustain frost for long, and its range corresponds approximately to the limit of the 0°C isotherm for minimum temperatures in the coldest month of the year. Natural boundaries like this can provide an indication of climate in those areas where there are no meteorological measuring stations.

variations in the weather from year to year. In summer, if the westerly circulation is at relatively low latitudes, the rainfall is high. On the other hand, if the subtropical anticyclonic belt is at high latitudes, the summer is very dry.

The Mediterranean climate on the western side

A remarkable feature of the Mediterranean climate is the absence of precipitation in summer. The length of the dry period increases towards the equator or as one moves eastwards: from three months in Nice, it becomes five months in Algiers, then nine months in Beirut. Annual precipitation, between 300mm and 1,000mm, occurs mainly in the cold season, but occasionally in autumn in the form of fierce, sometimes devastating downpours. The Mediterranean climate is generally very bright because of the small amount of cloud cover and high levels of sunshine.

Winter temperatures are usually mild, and frosts are rare. Summer temperatures become higher as one moves inland, away from the sea's moderating influence.

In the Mediterranean region, the vegetation is able to withstand dry summers. In some cases, the plants have glossy and sometimes hairy or prickly leaves, in order to limit water loss.

Of course, there are slight variations to this pattern, with certain features changing according to geography. For example, invasions of cold air become more frequent the higher the latitude, while summer droughts are more severe on the tropical margins. A certain continentality can be observed towards the east, whereas advections of humid air are more frequent in the west: on the oceanic margins (Morocco, Chile, South Africa), morning mists are quite common, even in summer.

The Chinese climate on the eastern side

Precipitation is relatively high in the Chinese climate, between 1,000mm and 1,500mm a year. It occurs throughout the year, but summer is the wettest season because of warm humid air masses that drift up from the tropical zone, carried by the trade or monsoon winds. The summer is hot. In winter, depressions from the polar front and even anticyclones from high latitudes can affect regions with this climate. When there is an invasion of polar air, the temperature can fall dramatically.

Mistral, bora, khamsin, sirocco

There is no wind system that is especially typical of the Mediterranean climate. However, perhaps because of the considerable aridity of these regions, dry winds are particularly strong: the mistral and the bora are cold dry winds associated with the mountains further to the north, while the khamsin and the sirocco are dry and hot, and blow from the desert further south.

The equatorial climate

Hot and humid, without marked seasonal contrasts, the equatorial climate is found near to the equator, where the length of the day is the same throughout the year.

Geographical limits

Despite what its name suggests, the equatorial climate is found not only at the equator itself, but also at latitudes of up to 10° or 20° in Central America, the Amazon Basin, the West Indies, Indochina and the Philippines. Nor does the whole band of the equator have an equatorial climate: for example, western Africa has very distinct dry seasons, and certain mountainous regions have topography that dramatically affects the climatic conditions at low altitudes.

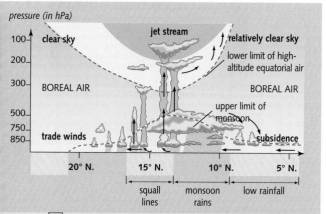

pressure (in hPa)

clear sky — jet stream — relatively clear sky — lower limit of high-altitude equatorial air

BOREAL AIR — BOREAL AIR — upper limit of monsoon

trade winds — subsidence

20° N. — 15° N. — 10° N. — 5° N.

squall lines — monsoon rains — low rainfall

The intertropical convergence zone is the boundary between the atmospheric circulation of each of the hemispheres. The trade winds, which develop on the sides of subtropical anticyclones, blow from north-east to south-west in the northern hemisphere and from south-east to north-west in the southern hemisphere: where they meet there is an ascent, characterized by cumulonimbus clouds, and a low-pressure belt surmounted by a jet stream.

Heat and humidity

The equatorial climate is hot and humid throughout the year. Average temperature is of the order of 26°C and annual amplitude is small, between 1°C and 6°C. It is generally smaller than daily amplitudes, which can reach 10°C. This degree of consistency encourages the growth of a multilayered evergreen forest.

Precipitation on the plains is between 1.5m and 2.5m a year, except on high ground exposed to humid winds: on Mount Pelée in Martinique, for example, at an altitude of 1,400m, there is 8m of precipitation during the year. In some areas, such as Indonesia and New Guinea, precipitation continues throughout the year, sometimes peaking slightly at the equinoxes. In other regions, like the Amazon Basin or the Congo, there is an embryonic dry season. As long as this does not exceed three months and the precipitation of the preceding months is sufficient to compensate for the deficit, this does not inhibit plant growth. Humidity, which is high all year round (always above 75%, and sometimes above 90%) is linked to the warm air and ready supplies of water provided by the ocean, the ground and the vegetation.

Supplies of sunshine and intertropical convergence

Regularly hot temperatures are the result of substantial, regular supplies of sunshine: there are 12 hours of daylight during which the Sun beats straight down, so the amount of solar energy received is high. However, because of the intensity of evaporation, the sky is very often cloudy and the Sun does not shine for half of its maximum theoretical duration, which limits the extent to which the ground warms up during the day and

The equator in climatology

In climatology and meteorology, scientists sometimes talk about the 'meteorological equator', meaning the line that separates atmospheric circulation in each of the hemispheres. But they also talk about the 'thermal equator': this is the imaginary line linking the maximum annual average temperature on each meridian. The 'cold pole', on the other hand, describes the region in each hemisphere where the lowest temperature has been recorded.

reduces cooling at night.

The large amount of precipitation is due to intertropical convergence. The regions which have an equatorial climate are those in the zone where the trade winds converge. In the wide band known as the intertropical convergence zone or 'meteorological equator', pressures are low, the thermal gradient is not very pronounced and it is easier for air to ascend. Since the intertropical convergence zone has a seasonal pattern of migration related to the effect of the general circulation of the atmosphere, the wettest periods are those when convergence is at its most active over the equator – in other words, at the equinoxes.

In the great forests of the equatorial zone, it is thought that the water cycle operates almost entirely in a closed circuit: evapotranspiration provides the necessary humidity, the heat enables moist air to rise and condense, and precipitation is triggered locally. However, advections of moist air are required to maintain the stock of water, part of which is carried away by rivers.

The tropical climate

> The tropical climate is characterized by the absence of a cold season and by one or two humid seasons with one or two dry seasons in between.

Two bands on either side of the equator

The tropical climate is found throughout the intertropical zone. However, it excludes arid tropical climates, which have a dry season lasting more than ten months and annual precipitation of less than 450mm. It also excludes climates whose dry season is not very marked: these fall into the category of equatorial climate. The tropical climate may be dry or wet to varying degrees. It is found at low latitudes, along two bands: the first, in the northern hemisphere, passes through Central America and northern South America, then through western and central Africa (the southern coasts of Senegal and the Gulf of Guinea,

Savanna vegetation is typically found in a tropical climate. The number of trees depends on the intensity and length of the rainy season.

as far as the Great Lakes), and finally through Asia, from India to Indochina. A second band, in the southern hemisphere, takes in the southern edges of the Amazon Basin as far as Paraguay, Angola, southern Zaire, Zambia, the western coasts of Madagascar, southern Indonesia and New Guinea, and northern Australia.

High temperatures

Temperatures are high in all these regions, the average for the coldest month being above 18°C. However, the temperature falls at night during the dry season in winter when the days are shorter: minimum temperatures of 12°C in Africa and 10°C in Asia are commonplace. But it is rainfall in particular that provides a seasonal pattern: there is generally only one dry season on the margins of the equatorial climate but, moving away from the equator, two dry seasons gradually become the norm. The first, more distinct dry season occurs during the winter, when nights are longer and the Sun is lower in the sky, so that it is sunny during the daytime but cool at night. The second dry season is shorter but more uncomfortable. It occurs in spring, and the

🐾 **Some trees** adapt to the dry season by developing enormous trunks, in which they store water until the humid season returns.

long parched days, when the Sun climbs high in the sky, can frequently produce temperatures of over 40°C.

The rainy season

The main rainy season is in the summer (August), although in Asia it is in the autumn (October to November). In north-eastern Brazil, it is at its height between June and August – winter in the southern hemisphere. Between 0.5m and 2m of water can fall during the rainy season. In many regions, there are two rainy seasons, one at the beginning of the summer and the other at the beginning of winter. This means that the tropical climate can be divided into two sub-climates: humid tropical (also called Sudanian) with a long rainy season of between seven and ten months and a dry torrid season which is less distinct; and dry tropical (also called Sahelian), with a very distinct dry season and more irregular rainfall. These patterns of rainfall should be seen in the context of the shifting intertropical convergence zone, where powerful ascents occur, encouraging precipitation to develop.

Seasonal shift

Like all atmospheric circulation, which is powered by solar energy, the intertropical convergence zone, or 'meteorological equator', undergoes a seasonal shift, extending and moving to a higher latitude during the summer. Thus, it moves north when it is summer in the northern hemisphere and south when it is summer in the southern hemisphere. In August it reaches its northernmost limit and around February its southernmost limit.

The monsoon climates

> The monsoon – a crucial element in rainfall patterns – is an
> atmospheric current that crosses the equator in the form of
> trade winds, changing direction at the same time.

From Africa to Australia, but especially in Asia

The monsoon occurs throughout the intertropical zone, except between 20° W (western coast of Africa) and 160° E (eastern Australia), where the winds do not change direction because the intertropical convergence zone is not crossed by the trade winds. It therefore occurs between East Africa and Asia, from the Indian Ocean to Australia and New Guinea. What all these regions have in common is a strong contrast between a continental landmass to the north and an ocean to the south. However, in Australia and Africa, the monsoon is not associated with a cold winter. This is why some people prefer to limit the term 'monsoon' to Asia, for it is on the Indian subcontinent that it is most intense.

The contrast between an overheated continent and a cooler ocean is one of the requirements for the development of a monsoon. The monsoon weakens when there is not such a great contrast between temperatures, which happens once the days grow shorter at the end of the summer.

Rains concentrated in a single season

From the point of view of temperature and precipitation, the climate patterns in India can be described as tropical, with a spring (April to May) that is dry and torrid. The rainy season begins in June or July, moving north and west, and ends in September or October when the monsoon wind moves away towards the south. This rainy season is very intense, with the regions concerned receiving more than 80%, and sometimes nearly 100%, of their annual precipitation. Then the dry season begins, and lasts until the following summer. In winter, the north-eastern monsoon starts, with air masses arriving over India from the Eurasian continent. These flow over the Bay of Bengal, gathering water on the way and producing some precipitation, mainly over the eastern Deccan. The light is generally very clear at this time of year, and sometimes the weather is cooler. In regions like northern Australia, on the other hand, where the winter monsoon has travelled over the ocean, it brings rain with it.

In South and Southeast Asia, more than 80% of the region's water is supplied by the monsoon. The downpours of water are often very heavy, and it is here that world records for annual precipitation have been set (more than 10m a year in the Himalayan foothills).

Unusual circulation of the atmosphere

In winter, the circulation of the atmosphere over South Asia follows the same model as for other regions: an anticyclone belonging to the tropical high-pressure belt covers the Indian sub-continent and generates north-easterly winds on its southern side. These winds are part of the trade-wind belt, and these trade winds cross the geographical equator. As they do so, they change direction: this is then known as the north-east monsoon. In winter in the southern hemisphere (summer in the northern hemisphere), the Indian Ocean anticyclone becomes stronger: the trade winds which have formed on its northern side are driven northwards well beyond the equator, because the Indian anticyclone weakens to the point of disappearing due to the warming up of the ground and the lower layers of the atmosphere. As it crosses the equator, the current changes direction: this is then known as the south-west monsoon. Over India, this current shifts once again when it encounters the Himalayas.

A word with several meanings

The word 'monsoon' comes originally from Arabic and refers to the annual change in wind direction over southern Asia and the Indian Ocean. But it is also used to describe the season when this wind occurs (usually the south-east monsoon season is referred to), as well as the air mass driven by this wind (monsoon rain) or this particular type of general atmospheric circulation. In some cases, the word is used to refer to the entire region where it is likely to occur; in other cases, it refers only to India, Southeast Asia and eastern Asia.

Climates that support life

E xtreme, or arid, climates restrict life: the lack of water is a limiting factor for vegetation, animals and humans. It is difficult to set a rainfall threshold for aridity, as it depends not only on precipitation, but also on evaporation, which in turn depends on air temperature, pressure and wind speed. Aridity can also be assessed by studying plants and animals. Even though life can be found over almost the entire globe, the variety and density of biological activity is greatly reduced and much more uniform in arid regions.

Minimal plant activity and diversity are good indicators of the way climate can restrict life. This is due to a lack of precipitation or to the cold, which causes a biological drought.

Extreme climates

The limiting factors of climate

Thanks to the atmosphere and its particular composition, the Earth has, on the whole, a climate that supports life. But sometimes there are factors that can restrict this.

Signs of life and human settlement can be found in both hot and cold deserts, but these signs are few and far between compared to places where the climate is more clement. This is due to the shortage of food supplies in deserts.

Individual limiting factors

Wind is rarely seen as a factor restricting life, but it can disturb plant growth or kill it off altogether if it reaches very high speeds. Plants adapt (by putting out deep roots, growing out of shape, etc), and this enables them to withstand most situations.

An absence of water is the most limiting factor where climate is concerned, because water is essential to life. But circumstances vary from place to place, and a region with low rainfall often has other water systems that are either inherited (such as deep groundwater) or active (streams and rivers). Living organisms can learn to adapt to these different situations.

Temperatures restrict life only in the most extreme cases – for example, in very hot regions where there is no humidity to compensate for the intense evaporation, or in icy regions which become arid because of the air's limited ability to contain water vapour. In such cases, it is the combination of temperature and humidity that actually sets the limits.

This Icelandic house has been covered with a layer of turf to provide thermal insulation. The direction the house faces has been chosen with the prevailing winds and exposure to the sun in mind.

Average and extreme situations

Living organisms develop on the basis of a climate's average conditions and reasonable deviations from these averages. Extreme situations, which only occur in rare instances, are restrictive – or at least seem so. For example, an exceptionally strong gale blowing over a tree plantation that is not used to such winds can cause huge short-term economic damage; however, most plantations have a great capacity for regeneration, and these exceptional events are matched by a recovery that is just as exceptional.

Civilization and the Ice Age

Climatic conditions during the Ice Age, 20,000 years ago, were harsh. At middle latitudes, temperatures were about 10°C lower than they are today. However, this period seems to have been a good one for prehistoric hunters, with varied and abundant wildlife in the cold steppes. The first artistic endeavours date from this period, too, and according to some theories the difficult conditions that prevailed forced people to group together and organize themselves in order to survive, thus triggering the dawn of a new civilization.

Stability and change

Although climate stability is seen as promoting stable living conditions and diversification, it can also be a source of weakness because the environment loses its ability to adapt. At the opposite extreme, a variable climate guarantees diversification by making the environment more adaptable. However, if climatic conditions change too rapidly, or if extremes of weather occur too often, the natural environment and living organisms are not able to make use of their natural ability to adapt, nor can they undertake the migrations necessary for self-preservation. In the long term, these changes will lead to new biotic environments.

Map (following pages)

The distribution of arid climates corresponds to areas of high pressure, which prevent advections of humid air and the ascent necessary for precipitation to develop. This is why arid climates can be found in the middle of the ocean. Aridity is also linked to continentality in so far as it is influenced by distance from any mass of water. Finally, there are coastal deserts that are created by cold oceanic currents.

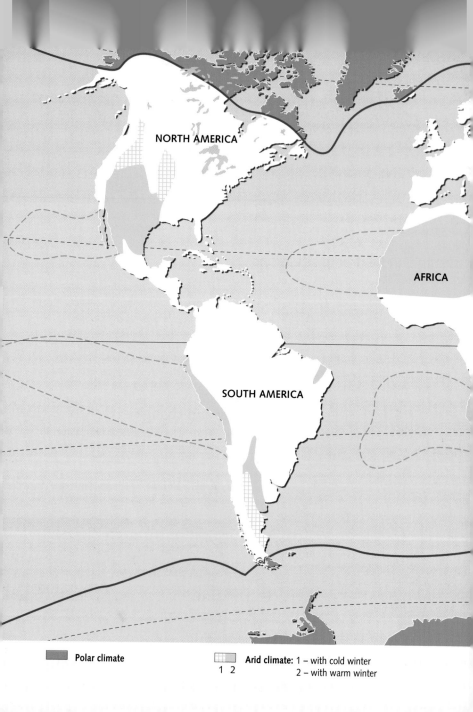

NORTH AMERICA

AFRICA

SOUTH AMERICA

Polar climate

Arid climate: 1 – with cold winter
2 – with warm winter

1 2

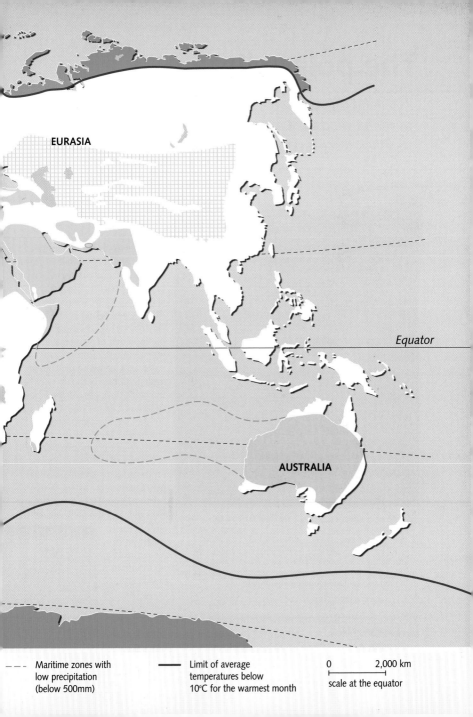

EURASIA

Equator

AUSTRALIA

- - - Maritime zones with
low precipitation
(below 500mm)

——— Limit of average
temperatures below
10°C for the warmest month

0   2,000 km

scale at the equator

The polar climate

The polar climate is arid, with cold summers, icy winters and powerful winds that reinforce the drying effect of the air. Taken together, these factors almost exclude any possibility of life.

Since weather stations are few and far between at very high latitudes, the polar climate has long been defined by the tree line, which corresponds quite well to the +10°C isotherm for the least cold month. But other criteria can also be used: for example, the extent of permafrost (frozen ground), or frost-free seasons of about 60 days. Tundra is the typical vegetation found in this climate.

The +10°C isotherm

The extent of the polar climate is marked by the +10°C isotherm for average temperatures for the least cold month. In the southern hemisphere, this boundary lies roughly along 50° S, but it is more irregular around the Arctic, varying between 50° N (Labrador) and 70° N (north-eastern Siberia and Alaska), and taking in all of Greenland, two-thirds of Iceland, the top edge of Scandinavia and the Northeast Territory.

Winter is permanently cold at these latitudes, with February being the hardest month. At the Eureka station in Canada (situated at 83° N), the average temperature in February is -37°C. The northern coastline of Eurasia is icebound, with the exception of a narrow strip on the edge of Scandinavia that benefits from the effect of the North Atlantic Drift. Summers are less cold, and the perimeter of the Arctic Ocean is free of ice. Nevertheless, no month is free from frost. The further one goes towards the poles, the more icy surfaces there are and the less precipitation there is. Annual snowfall is about 1m on the islands close to the polar circle and 5cm at the centre of Antarctica.

Polar bears are perfectly adapted to the intense cold of these regions: their fur and fat protect them, enabling them to get their food from the icy waters of the Arctic Ocean.

Slight differences

Within these limits, there are slight but noticeable differences between four climate types: the climate at the centre of the icecaps (Greenland, Antarctica), the continental Arctic climate (northern coasts of Siberia, Canada and Greenland), the oceanic polar climate (northern Scandinavia, islands off northern Scotland, Spitsbergen, south-western Greenland) and the oceanic subpolar climate (northern Iceland, southern tip of Greenland, islands in the southern Indian and Pacific Oceans). The first climate is permanently cold (-89°C in July 1989 at Vostok, in the centre of Antarctica); precipitation, which always falls as snow, is low. The second climate has a summer period accompanied by a strong thaw. The third climate has severe winter temperatures but a summer with several months of thaw and plentiful precipitation (300mm to 500mm). The fourth climate is milder: thawing is possible throughout the year and precipitation is very plentiful (500mm to 1,500mm a year) in the form of winter snow.

A factor of aridity

When temperatures are very low, they become an important factor in restricting biological processes. These restrictions operate in two ways. First, when freezing occurs, the water cycle changes, because a substantial proportion of the water stock is immobilized in the form of ice. Second, the temperature of the air has an impact on its humidity capacity: a maximum of $4.8g/m^3$ of water vapour at 0°C, and $0.34g/m^3$ at -30°C.

The polar anticyclone

These climate patterns are linked to the general circulation of the atmosphere: in winter, very low temperatures are a result of weak sunlight, which encourages the formation of a high-pressure zone preventing the advection of milder or more humid air. At a lower latitude, the westerly currents (particularly powerful in the southern hemisphere) bring humid air. In summer, sunlight weakens the high pressure, and disturbances circulating on the margins can penetrate areas that were inaccessible in winter.

The cold arid climate

Very little precipitation, low relative humidity, substantial amounts of sunshine, torrid summers, harsh winters – these are all typical of the cold arid climate.

Low, irregular precipitation

The cold arid climate is found on continental landmasses at middle latitudes in North America and, to a lesser extent, in South America and Argentina. But it is most extensive in Eurasia, spreading from the shores of the Black Sea through central Asia to Mongolia.

In these regions, precipitation is low and irregular. This is due to the fact that advections of sea air are few and far between, either because these regions are situated several thousands of kilometres from the ocean (Asia), or because they are shielded by a mountain barrier (North and South America). In certain regions, such as the plateaus of Tibet and Iran, both of these factors play a part. Precipitation is irregular except in semi-arid regions, where there is an embryonic rainy season. This is particularly true of regions east of the Caspian Sea, over which air masses carried by the western currents are able to regain their humidity: here, precipitation peaks in the spring.

Extreme continental climate

The extreme continental climate is found in vast stretches of North America and Asia north of 50°. It forms a transition between temperate continental climates, polar climates and cold arid climates, and is characterized by several dry, very cold winter months and a short summer without much rain, although it is often hot and stormy. Vegetation grows luxuriantly over the course of the summer. It is here that the greatest amplitude is found between the hottest month and the coldest month, with 62°C in Siberia. Precipitation remains meagre except in eastern areas where advections of humid air are more frequent. The ground is covered with a layer of snow for six to eight months, powerful anticyclones are present, and blustery winds blow in the form of blizzards or the buran.

Originally from central Asia, camels are very well adapted to aridity and cold: they store fat in their humps and can digest the toughest grasses.

High temperature ranges and drying winds

Naturally, temperatures depend on latitude: the further away from the equator one goes, the lower the average temperature. Daily temperature ranges are high. This is due to low air humidity and the absence of clouds, which is responsible for high levels of sunshine and a limited greenhouse effect: thus warming during the day and cooling at night are both

GLOSSARY

[Continentality]
The totality of the climatic changes relating to the diminishing influence of the sea, the further one goes into the interior of a continent.

accentuated. Annual amplitudes are more marked the higher the latitude, with hot summer days and icy winter days. This seasonal contrast is also linked to differences in amounts of sunshine, which are already noticeable at these latitudes. As for winds, all regions that are situated beneath mountains (the Andes, the Rockies, the Iranian plateau and the Pamirs) are liable to be affected by föhn-type winds with their formidable drying effects: the chinook in North America and the Afghan wind in central Asia are two cases in point.

Continentality

From an atmospheric point of view, drought can be explained first and foremost by geographical factors such as distance from the ocean or mountains that form a shield. The position of centres of activity reinforces these factors: in winter, high pressure restricts the advection of humid air, and in summer, low pressure may facilitate the arrival of masses of tropical air which have taken up more water from any existing inland seas.

Steppe vegetation is the vegetation type characteristic of a cold arid climate. It consists of tough grasses and other plants that are adapted to the cold.

The hot arid climate

This is a record-breaking climate, with hardly any rain and maximum amounts of sunshine. There are plants and animals in these regions, but they have adapted to very specific conditions.

Two belts at tropical latitudes

The hot arid climate is found at tropical latitudes in the northern and southern hemispheres, usually at the centre of continental landmasses (Mexico, the Sahara, the Horn of Africa, Arabia, the Iranian and Afghan plateaus and the Thar, Kalahari and Australian Deserts). It also develops in zones on ocean coasts (California, Chile, Namibia) and on islands off the coast (Cape Verde Islands, Easter Island).

Although extremely inhospitable, the hot arid climate does not exclude life totally. In restrictive circumstances like these, plant life shows just how adaptable it can be. Plants can survive for several years as seeds, waiting for a fall of rain before completing their reproductive cycle; some leaves are covered with soft fine hairs to limit evaporation; and taproots burrow deep into the soil to find water. Indeed, in the Sahara, 3,000 plant species have been recorded whose distribution is largely dependent on water availability.

The **fennec's** large ears help it to regulate its internal temperature, and it possesses highly developed nocturnal vision which allows it to move around during the coolest time of the day. This animal has adapted well to the inhospitable conditions of the hot arid climate.

Three degrees of aridity

The degree of aridity in these regions may be moderate (semi-arid climate), high (arid climate) or extremely high (hyperarid climate). In the case of a hyperarid climate, precipitation is always below 50mm a year and sometimes much less: at Aswan, in Egypt, the average annual precipitation is 2mm. In fact, the notion of average in this context no longer has much meaning, since rain can be absent altogether for several years in succession and then resume at any time of the year in the form of short heavy showers. As far as the strictly arid climate is concerned, average precipitation is between 50mm and 150mm a year and occurs more regularly. In the semi-arid (or subarid) zones, there is an embryonic rainy season of one to four months. Aridity becomes greater where continental landmasses are largest: the Sahara and the southern parts of Egypt and Libya have a hyperarid climate, while southern Algeria has an arid climate, and northern Algeria has a semi-arid climate.

Large amounts of sunshine and soaring temperatures

All of these regions are influenced by tropical high pressure, which is why aridity can also affect oceanic regions like the Cape Verde Islands. There are very large amounts of sunshine (it can reach 90% of its maximum theoretical value) and, because the angle of incidence of the radiation is almost perpendicular, the energy received is very substantial. Annual average temperatures are very high (25–30°C) with distinctive daily patterns: in the daytime, the temperature can rise to more than 50°C (Death Valley in California), but as soon as night falls, the temperature can drop by 30°C in a few hours (in winter, it regularly falls below freezing point). This is linked to low humidity and therefore to the greenhouse effect.

The coastal arid climate

Often more arid than neighbouring continental zones, coastal deserts extend northwards and southwards on the western sides of continents: for example, Atacama in northern Chile, Lower California, Namibia, southern Morocco and Mauritania. Most coastal deserts consist only of narrow strips of land, because mountain ranges such as the Andes and the Rockies border the coasts along which cold ocean currents flow (the Humboldt, California, Canary and Benguela Currents). These currents cool the lowest layers of the atmosphere. This cold humid air is topped by warm dry air at high altitude: the ascent necessary for (exceptional) precipitation to form is impossible. However, these conditions do encourage fog and very low clouds to develop. Consequently, there is only a small amount of sunshine, humidity is high and temperatures are less extreme than in continental deserts.

The climate of a place depends largely on its latitude and whether there are oceans or mountains nearby. But locally, climate is also influenced by other elements, such as the nature of the soil and the geological substratum, the local vegetation, the presence of rivers, lakes and ponds, and whether or not the area is inhabited. These various elements shape the climate by influencing the amount of sunshine, the water cycle, air circulation and temperature; and these in their turn shape the environment.

A small mountainous island can have a variety of local climates based on altitude, the proximity of the sea, and whether it is exposed to or protected from the prevailing winds.

Local climates

Soil, vegetation and continental waters

> The great forests and deserts have an influence on local climate, but they can also have a global influence when they extend over vast areas.

Vegetation

Plant life is very dependent on climatic conditions: sunshine allows photosynthesis to take place, while air humidity and rain promote growth. Temperature and wind also play their part in enabling plants to grow. Most plants bear the physical evidence of these factors, which sometimes act as constraints: for example, there may be rhizomes or bulbs which allow the plant to survive the inhospitable winter season, or leaves which develop aerial roots to avoid a surfeit of water.

Vegetation also influences climate through evapotranspiration, which can provide a not inconsiderable amount of water – indeed, it is always more humid in and around large forests. In the great Amazonian forest, for example, water is permanently being recycled: it rains, the plants absorb part of the water, which they then lose through evaporation or transpiration, and then it rains again.

The presence of water masses on a very local scale can noticeably change the climate: for example, mists can form which shut out the sun for several hours a day, or the humidity level can be raised, which has the effect of reducing temperature differences.

Surface formations

Climate plays an important part in determining rock formations and terrain, as well as in soil development. It is the main factor in erosion: rocks weather under the effect of rainwater, whose mild acids dissolve certain minerals; when it freezes, water can cause rocks to burst open; raindrops and hail can destroy surface layers; loose rocks or earth can be transported elsewhere by landslides, and so on.

However, climate is itself shaped by these same surface formations. Colour, for example, plays a part in determining the level of local radiation (reflection of radiation by means of the albedo), and therefore the capacity to store energy: a dark substratum absorbs more energy on the whole than a light substratum, and can restore this energy in the form of heat when it is coldest. In the same way, the ability of a material to retain water and then give it back affects the humidity of the air.

The purpose of micro-greenhouses like these is to 'improve' the local climate: by protecting plants from the cold while letting them benefit from the warmth of the sun, biological activity can be accelerated. But if they are used on too large a scale, micro-greenhouses can change the climate by pushing up the albedo – there is an increase in reflected radiation – and reducing the evaporation of soil water.

Continental waters

Groundwater, rivers, lakes and glaciers are of course very dependent on the rainfall that determines their regime (high and low waters, raising and lowering of water levels). In the case of glaciers, temperature affects thawing and determines whether they extend or retreat. Water masses enable air masses to regain humidity through evaporation. In the case of large surfaces of water, such as Lake Baikal or the American Great Lakes, the effect is similar to that of an inland sea. All water masses, the smallest ones included, have an impact on cloud cover: marshes and ponds often cause repeated and persistent mist and fog. Sizeable water masses can create thermal breezes: through differential heating of the water mass and the land, daily breezes develop, blowing water towards the land during the day and the reverse at night.

Map (following pages)

In Martinique, rainfall depends on the prevailing winds, which are the trade winds. These winds are full of moisture and blow over the north-east of the island, encouraging precipitation there. However, in regions that are situated downwind (around Saint-Pierre, for example), the effect of the föhn is felt: the air is drier, there are fewer clouds and therefore less rain. Precipitation also increases with altitude and this is particularly evident over the mountainous north of the island, which is wetter than the south.

Local climates: Martinique

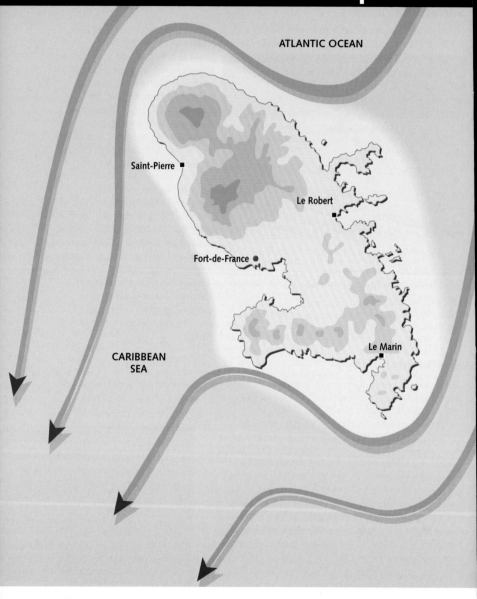

ATLANTIC OCEAN

Saint-Pierre ■

Le Robert ■

Fort-de-France ●

CARIBBEAN
SEA

Le Marin ■

Relief of Martinique

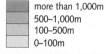

more than 1,000m
500–1,000m
100–500m
0–100m

Path of the trade winds over the Earth's surface
on either side of the island

0   10 km

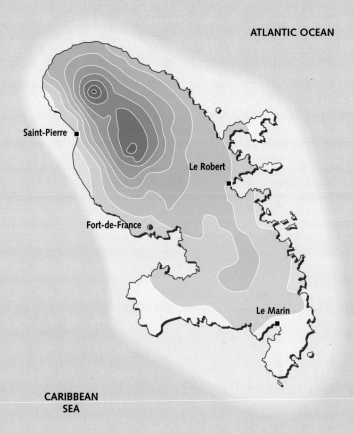

ATLANTIC OCEAN

Saint-Pierre

Le Robert

Fort-de-France

Le Marin

CARIBBEAN
SEA

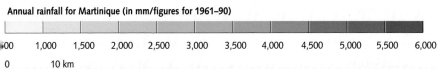

Annual rainfall for Martinique (in mm/figures for 1961–90)

00   1,000   1,500   2,000   2,500   3,000   3,500   4,000   4,500   5,000   5,500   6,000

0   10 km

Mountain climates

Even though mountains do not alter the main features of a climatic zone, they do effect changes by virtue of their altitude and exposure.

Altitude and exposure

The first change brought about by mountains is linked to altitude. As this increases, air density and atmospheric pressure decrease. Atmospheric absorption is reduced and solar radiation intensifies: at a height of around 3,000m at middle latitudes, the radiation is equivalent to the amount received on a plain at the equator. The second change is linked to exposure to the sun: at middle latitudes, the position of the mountain slopes in relation to each other is of prime importance, determining which are exposed to the sun and which are shaded (this is less important nearer the equator because of the almost vertical angle of incidence of the solar radiation). This leads to a range of small variations connected with temperature, humidity and precipitation.

A feature of mountain valleys at middle latitudes is the way vegetation grows in bands at different levels on opposite slopes. This is a result of the contrasts in climate between the slopes exposed to the sun and those in the shade. The climate also has an influence on the pattern of human settlement. Farming activities develop on the warm mountainsides, where the slope is gentler because of land-slides, whereas winter sports resorts are built on the cold, steeper slopes.

Cold pockets

The increase in radiation does not result in a higher temperature. Lowering of pressure and thinning of the air are now the determining factors, and these mean that the transformation of the radiation into heat by air absorption is reduced. The average temperature drop – around 0.6°C per 100m – varies slightly according to humidity, moving between 1°C per 100m (dry air) and 0.5°C per 100m (saturated air). Thus, mountains are cold pockets within the climatic zone they occur in. The situation varies from locality to locality, depending on relief, exposure and shading effects.

'Water towers' in the desert

Relief makes it easier for air to ascend, which is necessary for precipitation to develop. This ascent of air increases with altitude, both in quantity and intensity, until an altitude is reached where the rainfall peaks. The altitude at which this peak occurs depends on temperature and humidity, and it can be easily identified by the vegetation, which at this level will be ombrophilous forest. Beyond this altitude, absolute humidity drops very quickly, but the value of relative humidity varies greatly because of the range in temperature.

At low latitudes, the difference in vegetation at different levels is due to the decrease in temperature and to varying bands of humidity. This enables ombrophilous forests to develop, like the one seen here on the slopes of Mount Cameroon.

Exposure to the prevailing winds, especially if they are humid, produces a different effect: here, the slopes facing the wind are very wet, in contrast to the slopes that are downwind, which are dry and therefore almost barren. Finally, precipitation in the form of snow increases with altitude. The snow's strong reflective quality has an effect on radiation: temperatures drop and areas of relative high pressure set in over the highest mountains.

Sheltered sites, specific winds

Mountains provide both sheltered and windy sites, depending on their position in relation to the prevailing winds. But the variety of exposed situations and the effects of altitude produce very specific winds such as the föhn (a warm dry fast wind that blows on the sheltered side of mountain barriers) or thermal breezes. Temperature inversion also occurs in these situations: cold air accumulates in valley bottoms or steep-sided basins, capped by a layer of warm air that prevents any ascent. In such cases, the pollution level usually rises dramatically.

GLOSSARY

[Ombrophilous]
Adapted to high levels of humidity or rain.

Coastal and island climates

The particular feature of coastal and island climates is that they have large water masses nearby. This has consequences for humidity, sunshine, rain and wind.

Humidity and precipitation

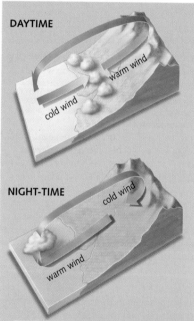

DAYTIME

warm wind

cold wind

NIGHT-TIME

cold wind

warm wind

Land masses heat up more rapidly and more intensely than water, which has high thermal inertia. During the day near the sea, the ground transmits heat to the air, which becomes lighter and rises, creating an on-shore breeze: a local ascending wind forms, and the colder sea air takes the place of the continental air. At night, the air cools more quickly on the land, and the current is reversed, moving from the land towards the sea in an off-shore breeze.

Usually, atmospheric humidity is high near coasts and on islands. Apart from areas with powerful anticyclones (the Cape Verde Islands, the Galapagos Islands, Easter Island) or coastal deserts (Atacama, California, Namibia), this high humidity encourages precipitation to develop, even if the rainfall regimes of the coast or island belong to a drier climatic zone. In addition to the high humidity, other factors also make precipitation more likely: orographic ascent over the continental landmass and a temperature contrast between ocean and continent. However, these factors sometimes do not come into play until a few kilometres inland; if this happens, then the immediate coastal strip is not necessarily very wet or experiences only light but persisitent precipitation in the form of drizzle.

Sunshine and temperature

Coastal and island regions generally have low levels of sunshine, high humidity and geographical factors which promote the condensation of water. Coastal regions are often foggy as well. However, here again, the coastal strip itself is not necessarily affected. Islands off the coast and the first few kilometres may receive greater amounts of sunshine than further inland.

Both near the sea and inland, daily and annual temperature ranges are low. This is due to the fact that water vapour acts as a moderating influence: humidity limits not only cooling at night and in the winter but also warming during the day and in the summer.

Coastal winds

Sometimes very specific winds develop near to the coast: these are known as coastal breezes. They are local or regional winds, often changing their character within the space of a day. They result from temperature differences in the lower layers of the atmosphere, which are caused by a difference in warming (or cooling) between the water and the land. In general, on-shore breezes appear in the morning, when the weather is still and sunny; they become stronger during the day and gradually die down at the end of the afternoon. Off-shore breezes get up around nightfall, dying down in the early hours of the morning. The on-shore breeze and the off-shore breeze are separated by a short interval when there is almost no temperature difference and the atmosphere is calm. Coastal breezes can be felt up to several kilometres from the coast.

Windward and leeward

Most islands have different degrees of exposure to the prevailing winds, with a windward side that experiences the full force of the wind and a leeward side that is protected from it. This contrast has a variety of implications for the climate. It means that the windward coast is generally wetter, while on the leeward side there are higher levels of sunshine, hotter temperatures and higher annual and daily temperature ranges. This has consequences for vegetation and land use, since – depending on which climatic zone the island is in – the windward coast can be unbearably humid, and the leeward side barren and inhospitable.

Even the most low-lying islands are prone to rising air and cloud formation. Such clouds are useful to navigators, enabling them to spot an island from a great distance.

Urban climates

The numerous components that make up towns and cities (buildings, streets, parks, etc) affect the climate, and promote the development of various microclimates.

The sun

Buildings create zones that are either overexposed to the sun on their south-facing sides or that mask it – some very confined spaces never see the sun, and indeed this is something that is favoured in hot countries, where houses are built close together to keep the sun out. Towns also have an impact on radiation. Roofs and walls usually have darker surfaces than vegetation; the albedo in a town is therefore weaker (between 14% and 19%, depending on building materials), and towns are good absorbers of solar radiation. In addition, pollution in the form of dust and gases reduces visible radiation and reinforces its absorption by the air.

The wind

By forming obstacles, buildings act as windbreaks and channel the wind, unlike open windy spaces. But whirlwinds, gusts and wind acceleration can also occur, particularly when the wind flow is restricted by buildings: for example at street corners, behind large buildings facing the prevailing wind, in the funnel created by two buildings close together, or in the open spaces between rows of houses on estates.

The more impenetrable the obstacle, the more forceful is the effect. Rows of houses in grid-shaped blocks often suffer more than neighbourhoods where the streets are laid out in an irregular fashion and the houses form small groups. But sometimes, particularly in hot countries, winds and breezes are welcome in a town, in which case the town can be built on a high point or headland, where it is windiest.

In calm weather, a warmer layer of atmosphere that is also richer in various pollutants hangs over towns and cities. This layer, which can clearly be seen from a plane when approaching a large city, is in the shape of a dome, or of a plume if it is deformed by the wind. Within this layer, it is easier for convection to take place and for air to ascend.

Temperatures

Temperature is affected by changes in the amount of sunshine and wind flow, but the most important factor is urban energy consumption: transport, heating, the lighting of public spaces and industrial activity, all of which give out heat. It is hotter in town than on the outskirts, especially if the weather is calm: differences of 2–3°C are commonplace. This produces thermal breezes, with the wind flowing from the colder outskirts towards the warmer town at night. The speed of these breezes is around 2–3m/s (7–10kph).

Precipitation

By diverting winds and causing particular movements of air, towns affect the local circulation of the atmosphere. Radiation phenomena (absorption, local greenhouse effect, etc) increase the instability of the air, causing it to rise and produce precipitation, which is higher on the leeward side of the town. But towns and cities themselves are often less wet, and this is due to the change in the water cycle brought about by making surfaces waterproof: the rain collects more rapidly and does not seep through. If the rain is very intense, this can have dramatic consequences.

Urban heat pockets are most in evidence in cold regions in winter: the difference between the centre and the outskirts can be as much as 10°C, although differences of 2–3°C are more usual. Frosts may be less frequent and some plants may flower early. This temperature contrast has several causes, including pollutants that reinforce the greenhouse effect, and combustion and lighting that give back heat.

Correcting the urban climate

Climate is a serious factor in urban planning, particularly where wind and precipitation are concerned. If not enough consideration was given to the effects of wind when a particular building was designed, then one solution is to set up windbreaks. The purpose of these is to slow down the wind by filtering it and gradually altering its course. As for precipitation, technical improvements can be made to reduce the risk of flooding (compensation basins, drainage channels, and surfaces that allow water to percolate back into the ground), or legal measures can be introduced: for example, making it obligatory to set aside some areas for vegetation so that water can seep away naturally.

Analysing climate change

Climate has become an important economic, environmental and political issue because of changes in the mixture of gases that make up the atmosphere – changes that could lead to a radical transformation of our climate.

Changes in the composition of the atmosphere

Apart from water vapour, 99% of the atmosphere is made up of oxygen and nitrogen. The remaining 1% consists of very small quantities of different gases, some of which are transparent in visible light but opaque under infrared radiation. These are known as greenhouse gases: mainly carbon dioxide (CO_2), methane (CH_4) and nitrous oxide (N_2O), which are naturally present in the atmosphere, and some new, totally artificial gases, such as CFCs and HCFCs. The concentration of many of these gases is steadily increasing – observations at the Mauna Loa station in Hawaii show that the amount of carbon dioxide has grown by 15% since 1960. Taking a longer timescale, samples taken by boring into glaciers in the Antarctic have enabled scientists to examine the history of the carbon dioxide content in the atmosphere over a

GLOSSARY

[CFCs]
Chlorofluorocarbons: synthetic gases made up of methane, ethane or ethylene, and propylene.
[HCFCs]
Hydrochlorofluorocarbons.

period of 160,000 years. They have shown that the carbon dioxide content has risen very noticeably since 1850 – about 30% over the course of a century, which is the fastest increase recorded during those 160,000 years.

The link between atmospheric composition and temperature

From the same Antarctic samples, scientists have also been able to reconstruct the history of atmospheric temperature over a 160,000-year period, which shows changes in temperature and gaseous composition are interlinked. This is quite normal, because greenhouse gases trap the Earth's infrared radiation and convert it into heat. This is why the planet's atmosphere naturally has an average temperature of 13°C: it would probably be -18°C without these gases and water vapour.

Source of greenhouse gases

Even though most of the gases involved in the greenhouse effect are naturally present in the atmosphere, the increase in their concentration is not entirely natural: it is connected

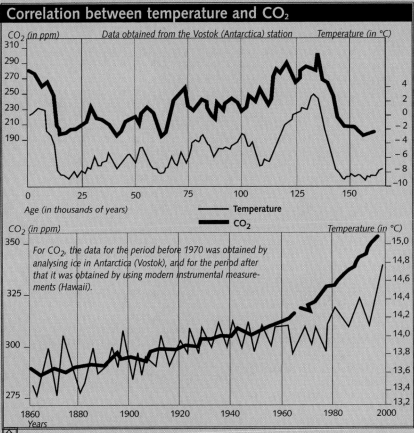

Correlation between temperature and CO₂

CO_2 (in ppm) — Data obtained from the Vostok (Antarctica) station — **Temperature (in °C)**

Age (in thousands of years)

——— Temperature
━━━ CO_2

CO_2 (in ppm) — Temperature (in °C)

For CO_2, the data for the period before 1970 was obtained by analysing ice in Antarctica (Vostok), and for the period after that it was obtained by using modern instrumental measurements (Hawaii).

Years

These graphs show measurements of CO_2 carried out at the Mauna Loa observatory in Hawaii, at an altitude of 4,000m, and measurements obtained from glaciological analyses at Vostok (Antarctica) using probes to a depth of 2,200m. The carbon dioxide content in the atmosphere and the air temperature over a 160,000-year period have been reconstructed by analysing air bubbles: the warmer the air, the more light isotopes it contains.

to human activity and, first and foremost, to energy consumption. By burning fossil fuels, we are depleting carbon that has been fossilized since the Palaeozic era. Industrial activity, transport and domestic consumption are responsible for the growth of carbon dioxide and nitrous oxide. Methane (CH_4) is linked to agriculture (the digestive processes of rumi-nants) and to land use (the decomposition of vegetation in marshland). CFCs and HCFCs have been used in aerosol sprays and refrigeration systems, but are being phased out by international agreement (the Montreal protocol). Water vapour is often linked to air temperature: the higher the temperature, the greater the evaporation.

Forecasting climate change

Our understanding of how the atmosphere works leads us to believe that its temperature will rise. What might the global consequences be?

Forecasting with models

In the same way that models are developed to forecast the weather over one, five or fifteen days, there are also models that simulate climate over longer periods. These are used to work out the degree and timescale of the likely climatic warming following a change in composition of the atmosphere. For example, if there were a doubling of carbon dioxide content, then temperatures might be expected to increase by between 1.9°C and 5.3°C. This would lead to an increase in evaporation and precipitation as well: perhaps between 3% and 15% for the latter. As for the timescale involved, it is thought that the 1850 levels of carbon dioxide will have doubled by between 2020 and 2100. The models also forecast the consequences of rises in temperature and precipitation on the icecaps and hence sea levels, if the icecaps were to melt: sea-level rises of between 14cm and 80cm would be expected between now and the end of the 21st century.

Uncertainty

These few figures are not sufficient to provide us with any degree of certainty. For instance, it is impossible to be sure about the role that an increase in cloud cover might play. More cloud cover would mean an increase in the planet's albedo, so that less direct radiation would reach the ground, and temperatures could drop. Similarly, many theories are being put forward about the way in which atmospheric and oceanic circulation are developing. What paths will depressions, cyclones and oceanic currents take? Will there be greater extremes of climate? The models do not provide forecasts in any great geographical detail, although new regional climate models are beginning to predict what local climates might be like at the end of the 21st century.

Uncertainty also surrounds the question of whether a major climate change has already begun. In the course of a century, the average temperature of the northern hemisphere has increased by 0.58°C, and the decade between 1990 and 2000 was the hottest since 1860, when the earliest reliable measurements were made. Close observation of glaciers reveals some of them to be melting (the Arctic and Antarctic ice floes have no effect on sea level, since ice floes float), while others (in Argentina and Chile) are growing as a result of increased snowfall.

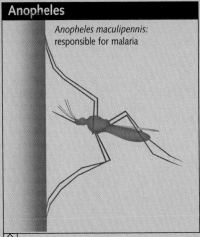

Anopheles

Anopheles maculipennis: responsible for malaria

Infections in birds in the Czech Republic, in horses in France, and deaths in the United States: for some years now, we have been witnessing a new spread of certain diseases usually transmitted by mosquitoes, such as the blue tongue virus in ruminants, the Ebola virus, and the Rift Valley fever virus. The growth in international travel and water engineering (for example, dam construction) may be partly to blame, but some people also see a link with climatic warming.

High stakes

The stakes are so high and the cost of climatic catastrophes so great that the issue has been taken up by politicians and economists. International agreements like the Kyoto Protocol are difficult for countries to adopt because the economic and social costs are high: they essentially demand a reduction in the consumption of fossil fuels.

Besides, not all countries are exposed to the same risks of climate change: the level of risk for a small island state in the Pacific is different from that for Russia, which has huge amounts of fossil fuels and may benefit from global warming.

Questions like 'How can emissions of greenhouse gases be reduced?' and 'Should we fear global warming or welcome it?' are different aspects of the same problem, and the stakes are high in each case. For island states like the Maldives or the Seychelles, global warming could result in their being submerged altogether. But for large northern countries like Russia or Canada, which are handicapped by long, hard winters, warming would make for a milder climate. There might then be a growth in agricultural production, a reduction in energy needs for heating or an improvement in the reliability of transport.

So much uncertainty, however, means that governments are forced to consider international agreements long and hard. Even supposing that advantages are to be gained from a changed climate, adapting to it will necessarily be costly: extensive areas of coniferous forest are not easily transformed into fertile plains. In the end, each country, for different reasons, must give serious thought to international agreements. Preventing major climate change is probably one of the most difficult challenges facing the world at the present time.

Simulations

In order to develop models, scientists regard the atmosphere as made up of superimposed layers, whose functions and interrelationships follow the laws of fluid dynamics and thermodynamics and can be simulated in mathematical equations. The precision and reliability of these models depend on how many initial factors are taken into account (information on the state of the atmosphere, the part played by oceans, vegetation, and so on), as well as on the spatial and temporal scales being considered. All this requires considerable computer capacity, which itself affects the reliability of the models – and, of course, interpreting these models is difficult, because we still have a very imperfect understanding of exactly how the atmosphere works.

Glossary

[Absorption]
Process by which a substance retains energy.

[Advection]
Horizontal movement of an air mass.

[Agroclimatology]
The application of climatology to agriculture.

[Air mass]
An extensive body of air, whose properties (temperature, humidity, etc) are relatively homogeneous.

[Albedo]
The ratio between the amount of radiation that falls on to a surface or body and the amount reflected. The albedo can vary according to the angle of incidence.

[Amplitude]
Difference between the minimum and maximum value of a set of data within a given time span (year, day, etc).

[Angle of incidence]
Angle formed between direct radiation and the surface receiving it.

[Aridity]
Situation in which potential evaporation always exceeds precipitation.

[Ascent]
Vertical upward movement of air.

[Average]
The sum of the values of a series of numbers divided by the number of values; in climatology, the average is calculated over a given period, which can vary between one day and a decade or more.

[Bioclimatology]
Branch of ecology that studies the relationship between living organisms and the climatic environment.

[Cell]
Atmospheric circulation generated by the differential distribution of energy sources, with vertical and horizontal motion in both the upper and lower troposphere.

[CFCs]
Abbreviation for chlorofluorocarbons; synthetic gases made up of methane, ethane or ethylene, and propylene. CFCs are involved in the deterioration of the ozone layer.

[Chlorofluorocarbons]
see CFCs

[Climate]
Combination of atmospheric states (temperature, wind, etc) in a given place and over a defined period (month, year, thousand years).

[Climatic anomaly]
Departure from the average of one or several climatic parameters which is of irregular occurrence and bears no comparison to extremes or seasonal excesses.

[Climatic crisis]
A climatic anomaly that is particularly strong and long-lasting, and that is linked to the atmospheric system's inability to regulate itself (El Niño is one of the best-known).

[Climatic parameter]
Atmospheric feature (sunshine, wind, air humidity, precipitation).

[Climatology]
A science whose purpose is to describe, classify and explain the distribution and history of different types of climate.

[Cloud cover]
Amount of cloud in the sky.

[Coalescence]
Process by which tiny droplets grow in size by colliding with one another.

[Cold pole]
Indicates the region in each hemisphere where the lowest minimum temperatures have been recorded.

[Condensation]
Transformation of water from a gaseous state to a liquid or solid state.

[Continentality]
The totality of the climatic changes relating to the diminishing influence of the

sea, as one goes further into the interior of a continent.

[Convection]
Transfer of heat in a fluid through the movement of molecules from a cooler, more dense region to a warmer, less dense region.

[Convergence]
Movement of two air masses towards the same point.

[Coriolis effect]
Alteration of the course of a wind or other moving body, due to the Earth's rotation.

[Dew point]
see Saturation point

[Diffusion]
Dispersion, by gases and atmospheric aerosols, of solar radiation in all directions.

[Disturbance]
A whirlwind system, usually of large dimension, characterized by a discontinuity between pressure fields, temperature and humidity.

[Divergence]
Outflow of air towards the exterior of the main flow.

[Drizzle]
Liquid precipitation made up of very fine water droplets (less than 0.5 mm in diameter), which fall while seeming to float in the air.

[El Niño]
An anomalous warming of the surface waters in the central and eastern Pacific Ocean, particularly along the Peruvian coastline.

[Evaporation]
Transformation of water from a liquid state to a gaseous state.

[Evapotranspiration]
The amount of water that evaporates into the atmosphere, either directly from the ground or through transpiration by plants.

[Fog]
Concentration of fine water droplets suspended near the surface of the ground (the term is used when horizontal visibility is equal to or less than 1km).

[Föhn]
A warm dry fast wind that is accompanied by a rise in temperature and increase in pressure. It blows on the sheltered side of mountainous areas.

[Fraction of sunshine]
Ratio between the observed duration of sunshine and its maximum theoretical duration. It is also known as 'fraction of insolation'.

[Front]
Zone of discontinuity (thermal, barometric, hygrometric) in the atmosphere.

[Fusion]
Transformation of water from a solid state to a liquid state.

[Geostrophic wind]
A horizontal wind whose direction and speed are determined by a balance between the force of the Earth's rotation (Coriolis force) and the atmospheric pressure gradient.

[Hygrometry]
Measurement and study of the water vapour contained in the atmosphere.

[Ice age]
A geological period during which the icecaps extended as far as the low latitudes and mountain glaciers spread into valleys.

[Instability]
The property of a system (air mass, for example) whereby any disturbance introduced into it tends to increase.

[Intertropical convergence zone]
Line separating the atmospheric circulation of each of the hemispheres. Also known as the 'meteorological equator'.

[Irradiation]
Quantity of radiant energy received by a surface.

[Isobar]
A line joining points of equal atmospheric pressure.

[Isotherm]
A line joining points that have the same temperature over a given period of time.

[Jet stream]
High-speed wind circulating in the atmosphere at an altitude of more than 6km.

[Latent heat]
The energy absorbed or released by a substance when it undergoes a change of state (fusion, vaporization, condensation).

[Maximum]
Term given to the highest value in a series of values over a given length of time; an average can be calculated based on daily, monthly or other maximum readings.

[Meteor]
A phenomenon observed in the atmosphere (precipitation or optical and electrical phenomena) with the exception of clouds.

[Meteorological equator]
see Intertropical convergence zone

[Meteorology]
Science of the atmosphere which studies atmospheric states, the main objective being to produce weather forecasts.

[Mist]
Light fog that reduces visibility to between 1km and 5km.

[Model]
Simplified or digitized representation of the atmosphere and its properties, used to forecast weather or simulate climate.

[Normal]
Statistical value of a climatic parameter, determined over a 30-year period.

[Ombrophilous]
Adapted to high levels of humidity or rain.

[Palaeoclimate]
Climate of the past, usually one from an earlier geological period.

[Photosynthesis]
The process whereby plants convert water, atmospheric carbon dioxide and solar radiation into organic matter.

[Pluviometry]
Study of rainfall, its characteristics, its distribution in time and space, and the techniques for measuring it.

[Precipitation]
All hydrometeors, whether liquid or solid, emanating from the atmosphere; all processes from water vapour condensation to rain or snow falls.

[Radiation]
Process by which energy is transported in the form of particles or electromagnetic or acoustic waves.

[Rainfall]
Amount of precipitation that falls in one place during a given period of time.

[Rainfall equator]
Line linking the rainiest points of the intertropical zone.

[Rainfall gradient]
see Thermal gradient

[Reflection]
Change in direction of incident radiation when it reaches a reflective surface, without change of wavelength.

[Regime]
Rhythm adopted by a climatic element (precipitation, temperature, etc) on a seasonal scale.

[Relative humidity]
Ratio of the mass of water vapour contained in a given volume of air to the maximum mass of water vapour that this volume of air could contain at the same temperature and pressure (expressed in %).

[Resultant wind]
Vectorial average of all wind directions and speeds for a given level, place and period of time; obtained by calculations based on the wind components.

[Saturation]
Maximum mass of water vapour that can be contained by a volume of air

at a given temperature and pressure.

[Saturation point]
Degree of atmospheric humidity required for an air mass to become saturated at a given temperature and pressure (also known as 'dew point').

[Sensible heat]
Heat which changes the temperature of bodies.

[Sheltered site]
Site that is protected from extremes of climate by an obstacle (vegetation, building, relief) of any size.

[Subsidence]
Vertical downward movement of air.

[Supercooling]
The state of water when it remains liquid although its temperature, or the external temperature, is below 0°C.

[Thermal equator]
Imaginary line linking the highest average annual temperature on each meridian.

[Thermal gradient]
Rate of temperature variation on a horizontal or vertical plane (also known as 'rainfall gradient').

[Troposphere]
Lowest layer of the atmosphere.

[Turbulence]
Instability of a swirling fluid, superimposing itself upon the moderate movement of the air.

[Water cycle]
The total water circulation between the various reservoirs on the Earth.

Useful addresses and websites

American Meteorological Society, 45 Beacon Street, Boston, MA 02108-3693, USA
This major American society produces a range of popular and professional journals.

Climatic Research Unit, University of East Anglia, Norwich NR4 7TJ
An important centre of climate research, especially concerned with the impact of climate change on the environment.

Journal of Meteorology, PO Box 5161, Bournemouth, Dorset BH10 4WJ
A popular monthly meteorological journal established in 1975.

Meteorological Office, FitzRoy Road, Exeter, Devon EX1 3PB
The 'Met Office' is a world leader in the provision of advice on the weather and the natural environment. The National Meteorological Archive and Library is situated at the Exeter headquarters.

Royal Meteorological Society, 104 Oxford Road, Reading, Berkshire RG1 7LL
This major British society has both professional and amateur members. Meetings are held on all aspects of the weather, and several journals are produced by the Society, including the popular monthly *Weather*.

www.ametsoc.org
The link to the American Meteorological Society online.

www.greatweather.co.uk
A very useful portal to many sites detailing current weather and forecast weather, particularly in the UK and Europe.

www.metoffice.com
Includes rainfall radar displays and many forecasts for different time periods. Very useful as a resource for students and teachers.

www.royal-met-soc.org.uk
The Society's website has useful links to many state meteorological services, as well as two sites for amateur meteorologists.

www.torro.org.uk/
A good source of information on storms, especially in the UK.

www.weathercharts.org
Weather charts and satellite pictures from around the world, regularly updated.

www.wmo.ch/index-en.html
The link to the World Meteorological Organization and all its activities.

www.worldclimate.com
What the weather is normally like at thousands of places worldwide.

Newsgroups

www.ukweatherworld.co.uk
Includes several forums in which world weather is discussed.

www.weather.org.uk/resource/newsgrps.htm
Up-to-the-minute chat about the weather and how it is changing.

Suggestions for further reading

Burroughs, W, *Climate: Into the 21st Century*, Cambridge University Press, Cambridge, 2003

Cox, J D, *Weather for Dummies*, John Wiley & Sons, New York, 2002

Dunlop, S, *A Dictionary of Weather*, Oxford University Press, Oxford, 2001

Dunlop, S, *How to Identify Weather*, Collins, London, 2002

Eden, P, *The Daily Telegraph Book of the Weather*, Continuum International Publishers, London, 2003

Harding, M, et al, *Weather to Travel*, 2nd edn, Tomorrow's Guides, London, 2001

Henson, R, *The Rough Guide to Weather*, Rough Guides, London, 2003

Lynch, J, *Wild Weather*, BBC Books, London, 2002

Mayes, J and Hughes, K, *Understanding Weather*, Hodder Arnold, London, 2004

Pearce, E A and Smith, C G, *Hutchinson World Weather Guide*, revised edn, Helicon, Oxford, 2002

Index

Illustration credits

Photographs

Cover image © Jeremy Woodhouse, Getty Images; 1 © Ciel et Espace/ASA/GSFC; 4 & 5 © J Head/SPL/Cosmos; 6 © NASA/SPL/Cosmos; 8 & 9 © Galaxy Contact/Explorer; 10 © ESC/SPL/Cosmos; 11 © J-F Lanzarone/Hoa-Qui; 14 © Lauros/Giraudon/Bridgeman Art Library; 15 right © SPL/Cosmos; 17 bottom © Jacana; 17 top © CTK/Camera Press/Gamma; 18 © P Le Floch/Explorer; 19 © H Morgan/SPL/Cosmos; 20 © C Boisvieux/Hoa-Qui; 21 © P Menzel/Cosmos; 22 © Bibl. Sainte Geneviève/Dupif Photo Studio; 23 © SPL/Cosmos; 24 & 25 © Ciel et Espace/Nasa; 31 © Nasa/SPL/Cosmos; 32 © SPL/Cosmos; 33 © Ciel et Espace/Nasa; 35 © Nasa/SPL/Cosmos; 36 © Météo France; 37 © Didier Cauvin; 38 © Nasa/SPL/Cosmos; 40 & 41 © Ciel et Espace/Nasa; 42 © H T Kaiser/Cosmos; 43 © R Mattes/Explorer; 47 © P Bertrand/Hoa-Qui; 49 © Zefa-TH-Foto/Hoa-Qui; 51 © P Bertrand/Hoa-Qui; 52 left © S Shaver-STF/AFP; 52 right © W Buss/Hoa-Qui; 55 © D Nunuk/SPL/Cosmos; 56 & 57 © Hervé Vincent/Avecc-Rea; 58 © J Poulard/Jacana; 59 © D Parker/SPL/Cosmos; 62 © European Space Agency/SPL/Cosmos; 63 © Galaxy Contact/Explorer; 65 © G Martin-Raget/Hoa-Qui; 66 © Data: International Satellite Cloud Climatology Project (ISCCP); processing: CNRS dynamic meteorological laboratory; design G Beltrando (Denis-Diderot University); 67 top © L Thorel/Jacana; 67 middle © S Cordier/Jacana; 67 bottom © E Valentin/Hoa-Qui; 69 © AKG Paris; 71 © J-L Dugast/Hoa-Qui; 74 & 75 © J & P Wegner/Jacana; 76 © R Bezjak/Focus/Cosmos; 77 © Sipa Press; 80 © P Stritt/Hoa-Qui; 81 © D Lefranc/Explorer; 82 © Ziesler/Jacana; 83 © F Zvardon/Jacana; 84 © E Valentin/Hoa-Qui; 85 © P Pilloud/Jacana; 87 © C Farhi/Hoa-Qui; 88 © C Champigny/Cosmos; 89 © J-D Joubert/Hoa-Qui; 91 © R Bezjak/Focus/Cosmos; 92 & 93 © Sipa Press; 94 top © T Dressier/Jacana; 94 bottom © Serena/NF/Hoa-Qui; 95 © Serena/NF/Hoa-Qui; 98 © T Walter/Jacana; 99 © S Cordier/Jacana; 100 © P Le Floch/Explorer; 101 © Zefa-Poelking/Hoa-Qui; 102 © G Gasquet/Hoa-Qui; 103 © Mero/Jacana; 104 & 105 © Th Denis-Huot/Hoa-Qui; 106 © D Scott/Jacana; 107 © F Perri/Cosmos; 110 © Egers/Jacana; 111 © Steinmetz/Cosmos; 113 © D/Faulkner/PHR/Jacana; 114 © Ph Renault/ Hoa-Qui.

Drawings and computer graphics

Archives Larousse, Laurent Blondel, Graziella Boutet, Jean-Yves Grall, Vincent Landrin, Tom Sam You, Léonie Schlosser
The publishers would like to thank Météo-France for supplying information for the annual rainfall chart for Martinique on pages 108-9 (source: Atlas climatique, le temps à la Martinique, Météo-France – Direction Interrégionale Antilles-Guyane, Fort-de-France, 1999).

For the English-language edition:

Translator
Rosemary Rodwell

Consultant
Dr Allen Perry
Department of Geography
University of Wales Swansea

Editor
Camilla Rockwood

Prepress
Kirsteen Wright

Prepress manager
Sharon McTeir

Publishing manager
Patrick White

Originally published by Larousse as *Petit atlas des climats*
by Laure Chémery

© Larousse/VUEF, 2003

English-language edition
© Chambers Harrap Publishers Ltd 2004
ISBN 0550 10158 6

Typeset by Chambers Harrap Publishers Ltd, Edinburgh
Printed in France by IME, Beaume-les-Dames